NIRMALA'S EDIBLE DIARY

NIRMALA'S EDIBLE DIARY

A Hungry Traveler's Cookbook with
Recipes from 14 Countries

BY

NIRMALA NARINE

CHRONICLE BOOKS
SAN FRANCISCO

Library of Congress Cataloging-in-Publication Data available.

ISBN 978-0-8118-6906-5

Manufactured in China

Designed by The Heads of State and Suzanne Fee
Typesetting by Jason Kernevich and Suzanne Fee
Food photographs by Diana DeLucia.

10 9 8 7 6 5 4 3 2 1

Chronicle Books LLC
680 Second Street
San Francisco, California 94107
www.chroniclebooks.com

ACKNOWLEDGMENTS

Thanks to my mom and dad; my brothers Kishore, Rudy, and Visho; and my sister-in-laws. My brilliant nephew David, his wife Nehal, and cutie Isha. My nieces Nadine and Nadiya and my prince Shane.

My dearest friends Ben Gutkin, Barbara Berger, and Alex Liu. I am forever grateful to you and all the things you do for Nirmala's Kitchen. Tifphani White, you still have the Nubian Queen title. My Tiger Lily, Laurie Holz, you are a true inspiration and a woman with such a unique soul.

My King Edward, you are my ballast and bliss to watch. You fill me with immeasurable joy with your singing, your jokes, your meticulous explanations of sports, and your stimulating logic on life; Mariska Hargitay.

The gracious and humble Mr. Bill LeBlond; Amy Treadwell and Sarah Billingsley—the goddesses with eight arms. Designer extraordinaire Vanessa Dina (aka my cowgirl) and Anne Donnard, both blessed with the power of foresight. The divine, delightful yet so delicious Mr. David Hawk and the incomparable and brilliant Mr. Peter Perez, thanks for believing in me.

To all who worked on this book, my heartfelt thanks to Diana DeLucia, Corrine Bernstein, Maureen Luchejko, Cayenee Fusco, Ray Bradley, Bridget Fitzpatrick, and Tara Lane for all your valuable time and patience.

To an extraordinary group of people at the NASFT who always make us at Nirmala's Kitchen so welcome at every show, the suave Mr. Bill Lynch, my girl Nancy Devlin, Chris Nemchek, Bill Smith, Jim Spencer, Cherif Moujabber, Donoto Cinelli, Brian Sullivan, and Mike Stella.

And to some of New York's bravest, Jim Carney, Dan Sullivan, Brendan Hagan, Mike Horan, Brian Burik, Don Capitali, Jim Tarrant, Dan Kudlak, in memory of Al Kahler, a veteran of these shows, and of our country.

A millions thanks to friends and colleagues near and afar, the inspirational Mr. Michael Chapman, Joan Bussdieker, Rob Webber, Rochelle "Rocky" Scott, Fiona Wong, Nana Adae, Marsha Echols, Gerry Shamdosky, Anthere Montayne, Phyllis Mintz, Carilyn Jennings, Erika Sipos, Roger Grant, Felix Villa, Paul Romanelli, Anna Wolfe, Yuri Laubach, Beth Pomper, Cheryl Slocum, Ron Tanner, Chris Crocker, Ken Seiter, Nancy Hopkins, Gayatri Iyer, Hyman Hacker, Deena Merlen, Richard Chin, Antonio Gonzales, Andrea Moudakis, Ann Daw, Paul Naraine, Sharon Chiddick, Kerry Nolan, Bruna Rondinelli, Bart Schmidt, Mary Ann Schultz, Jasper and Iona White, and Danielle Barbaro.

✻ ✻ ✻

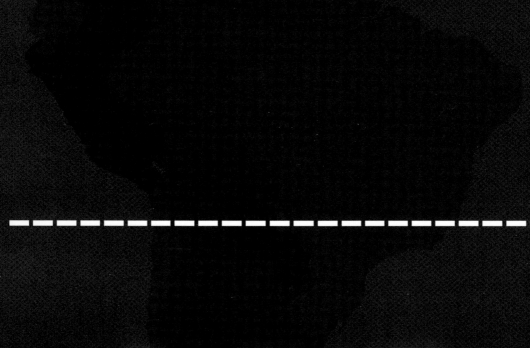

SOUTH AMERICA

CONTENTS

introduction

As a child, my entire world was a tiny village in Guyana, South America. I grew up with no running water or electricity, and, for Heaven's sake, I did not know about television.

My mother tells me that I was born on our kitchen floor on top of an empty wheat-flour bag, which she tirelessly washed to make into a soft bedsheet. Hours prior to my birth, she was at our farm, harvesting eggplants for the market. Apparently, the village midwife who delivered me while puffing away on her marijuana-filled pipe said, "Reenie! Dis child comin out cause dem heavy eggplant yuh fetch! It push she out fast, fast!"

The first food to grace my palate was not my mother's breast milk but mashed-up rice pudding spiced with cloves and Indian long pepper. It was an offering my grandmother had made to the Hindu gods for my arrival into this world. I had the leftovers.

As I reminisce about my childhood, I realize that I was truly cultivated for what I am today. The foundation for my adventure into the food and cultures of the world was laid by my guru—my grandfather—an Ayurvedic scholar and Hindu priest. Along the way, my culinary education was also nurtured by many schoolteachers who were descendents of African slaves and native Arawak Indians; and numerous Chinese, Javanese, and Portuguese cousins dotting the South American landscape. Of course, there were also my parents, who toiled in the farms under a hot Amazonian sun. My brothers and I were all destined to be farmers, since we were experts on sprouting seeds and building irrigation systems on our rice plantations. My childhood in Guyana began my creative journey into food, an early entry into the culinary travelogue of my edible diaries.

At the age of ten I came to America, where I blossomed in my new home in Queens, New York. My uncle, who served two tours in the Vietnam War, sponsored us. He, like my parents, did not want the hard life of farming for me and my three brothers. They wanted us to have an education and to live the American dream. The borough of Queens houses every ethnic culture from around the world. It was here that another branch of my journey into language, food, and culture began.

America, my new home, is where I was educated and then later worked in the corporate world. Preferring travel to work, I quit my day job and, during the past twenty years, I have traveled to more than 125 countries—and I never had qualms about being a woman traveling alone.

It was during my travels that the root of my passion—the interweaving of food and culture—resurfaced and inspired me to create Nirmala's Kitchen, a gourmet-foods company that brings global ingredients to home cooks, fusing cultures through food. Through our efforts, home cooks, busy moms, and adventurous gourmets don't have to leave the comforts of home to experience unique global flavors.

For me, writing about South America is like lifting the veil of my home continent. Wanting to give home cooks a glimpse of the riches of the food, cultures, and people of our southern neighbor, I write from the unique perspective of a citizen of both continents. There is nothing "exotic" or "Latin" about the ingredients in South America. In fact, what we in the States see as traditionally "American"—like potatoes, tomatoes, and corn—are actually indigenous to South America. South Americans love their meat as much as we do. With their staples being virtually the same as ours, many of the ingredients in these recipes can be found at your favorite market. And I include numerous options for alternative ingredients for items that are harder to find.

The culinary treasures and cooking techniques of South America remain largely unknown outside of its boundaries because that region of the world has done very little to export its authentic cooking traditions. The continent of my origin might be Latin dominant but part of its culinary secret is that it is home to people from many nations around the globe—and therefore their foods.

I truly believe that to experience the culinary delight of a culture you have to get to know the people. I have journeyed off the beaten path throughout South America, combining the discovery of traditional cultures, the splendor of the natural landscapes, and rekindled childhood memories.

My recipes are inspired by families, local villagers, farmers, food-stall vendors, orphans, bustling markets, and lush green plantations. I discovered that North and South Americans of many countries share dishes but refer to them in different languages. And what transforms these recipes into something unique are a few ingredients with which we are already familiar. My recipes reflect the multiethnic landscape of South America and home cooks may appreciate the easy-to-follow recipes and relatively inexpensive ingredients.

Please join me on a culinary journey through South America. Each chapter presents a different country and contains a brief country overview, along with recipes and excerpts from my personal travel diary. I will teach you how to use ingredients found at supermarkets, putting a new twist on meals and cooking methods. For example, you'll find the Italian influences of lasagna from Venezuela called *pasticho* made with a béchamel-like sauce of Parmesan cheese, spicy sausage, and coconut milk. Or the Welch-style cottage pie from the Falkland Islands with a hint of curry powder. Then there are *picarones*: sweet potato–donuts from Peru. And my favorite: passion fruit jellies from Brazil.

In the pages that follow, I share my childhood meals such as vichyssoise soup, made by my auntie in French Guiana, that is composed of taro, shallots, and coconut milk; the *cachaça* and blood–orange baked Christmas turkey from my Auntie Nevis in Brazil; Javanese spicy noodles from Suriname; and my family's influences of wonderful traditional spices brought over by my great-great-grandparents from India.

My travel pictures will tell another story, transporting you into the homes, farms, and markets of cooks just like you and me.

I am not a chef, and I don't like to be called one. I am a simple woman who loves to cook. A confession: I don't like to cook a meal for myself, but cooking for others? There is no greater purpose in my life. And I feel fulfilled when I can cook for entire villages or hundreds of orphaned children, like I do when I am traveling around the world.

In this book, I want you to see the diverse cultures, traditions, cooking techniques, and ingredients, along with memorable stories, from my South America. The continent is vast, and the people are hospitable, lively, and proud. I cannot possibly cover it all, but I hope you will allow me to share with you just a few pinches and dashes of my edible diaries.

❋ ❋ ❋

ingredients

AJÍ AMARILLO

Common in Bolivian and Peruvian dishes, these chiles have a light, fruity aroma but with a kick. They are mainly used to season potatoes, seafood, and wild game. They are available in Latin American groceries or specialty-foods stores in powdered or dried form, or you can buy them frozen.

ANNATTO

Also known as *achiote*, these tiny, square-looking seeds have a slightly fruity aroma and taste a bit peppery. Annatto is mainly used for the red color it imparts to soups, cheeses, rice, oil, and desserts. It is widely used in Mexican, Latin, and Caribbean cooking. You can buy annatto in well-stocked supermarkets. It is available in powdered form, whole, or as a paste.

AVOCADO

The avocado is also known as the "alligator pear" because of its shape and leathery skin. The pulp of this fruit can be enjoyed in a tossed salad or salsa, or sprinkled with a pinch of salt. The flavor is slightly buttery with hints of green tea. Several types of avocado can be found in most supermarkets.

CACHAÇA

The famous drink in Brazil, *caipirinha*, is made with *cachaça* liquor. *Cachaça* is made from fresh sugarcane juice that's been fermented and distilled. It differs from rum, which is usually made from molasses, a by-product from refineries that boil the cane juice to extract as much sugar as possible.

CARICA

This yellow fruit is found in jars at specialty-foods shops or online stores. It tastes like mangoes and papayas, and is used in desserts, sauces, and drinks. The *carica* plant is native to Central and South America. If a recipe calls for *carica*, you can use firm, ripe papayas.

CASSAREEP

Cassareep is a condiment made by boiling the juice of the cassava or yucca root. Spices and brown sugar are added to give it the taste of burned molasses with peppery spices. It's the essential ingredient in pepper pot soup. It can be found in West Indian markets.

CASSAVA

See Yucca.

CHAYOTE

Found in supermarkets everywhere, chayotes look like pears but with a rough, thin green skin. It is a bit bland, like unripe melon. The single seed inside and the skin are both edible. The chayote's white flesh is commonly used in salads. It can be stuffed, boiled, baked, fried, or pickled.

CUBAN OREGANO, INDIAN BORAGE, BROAD-LEAF OREGANO

Although this herb has many names, it has a singularly distinctive taste, and it smells like a combination of regular oregano and thyme. Its broad leaves are thick and meaty, and it adds wonderful spicy notes to almost any dish. It's popular in Cuba and other Caribbean countries as well as parts of South America. This herb grows easily and can be found at West Indian, Indian, and some Latin stores.

DENDÊ OIL

This bright-orange oil is a staple in Brazilian cuisine. Harvested from the nut of a palm tree, *dendê* oil is very high in saturated fat. Annatto oil is a substitute, as it imparts the red color without the fat. As for flavor, there is no difference. Both are found in Latin stores.

FEIJOAS

Feijoas are also known as "pineapple guavas" because of their flavor when ripe. This sweet, aromatic fruit is very juicy. It looks similar to a guava but its shape is more like an egg. It is used in drinks, desserts, and jams and can be found at specialty markets and Latin stores.

GUAVAS

This oval or round fruit has small, edible—but hard—seeds inside. The guava emits a sweet, pungent fragrance. Its flesh is white, red, or salmon-colored, and its flavor is a fusion of overripe strawberries and pineapples. The juice is used to make alcoholic drinks or shakes, and the pulp is made into jams. All versions can be found in supermarkets.

HUACATAY (BLACK MINT)

This native Peruvian herb has an aroma between marigold flowers and cilantro. The leaves are long and pointy, just like marigolds, and are ground to make a green paste. It is used on fish, seafood, and wild game. Huacatay can be found in paste form in Latin or Mexican stores, where it is called "Mexican Marigold."

MALAGUETA CHILES

These small, tapered chiles are found in Brazil and other South American countries. They turn red as they mature and only grow about 2 inches in length. It is a very hot pepper and is sometimes called *malaguetinha*. But don't get this chile confused with *melegueta* pepper (which is from the carda-mom family and is indigenous to Africa. *Malagueta* chiles are available in jars at Brazilian and some Latin stores.

MAUBY

This bark is widely used to make beverages. It is an acquired taste; initially sweet, somewhat like root beer, but then comes a bitter aftertaste. *Mauby* can be found in plastic bags in West Indian and Latin stores.

NARANJILLA

Also called *lulo*, this orange subtropical fruit has green juice and pulp, which are used to make drinks, sherbets, jams, and sauces. The flavor has notes of lime, rhubarb, and strawberry. Packages of *naranjilla* pulp can be found in the freezer section of Latin stores and some major supermarkets.

OKRA

This green vegetable is also known as "lady fingers." It's typically 3 to 4 inches long. Shunned by many for its mucilaginous qualities, properly cooked okra can be enjoyed by all. Many cooks claim the best method for producing delectable okra is to bake it. It can also be fried, stuffed, or cooked in soups or curries. Okra is available at local supermarkets, especially in the summer.

HEARTS OF PALM

Hearts of palm are cultivated from young palm trees. The bark is split open, exposing the layers of white fibers around a center core. Hearts of palm are often eaten in salads or tossed into soup. The flavor is like bamboo shoots with a hint of sweetness. They can be found in cans at specialty markets and Latin stores.

PASSION FRUIT

About the size of a medium lime, the passion fruit has a leathery, purple-brown skin that becomes wrinkled when the fruit is ripe. Its yellowish pulp is tart with a lemony flavor, and it is used in drinks and desserts. The black seeds inside are edible. Passion fruit can be found at local supermarkets.

PISCO

Pisco is distilled from a variety of grapes, and is the preferred liquor in Peru and Chile. Its aroma is faint but packs a potent punch. Pisco is never served straight up but rather is mixed with a variety of ingredients, such as citrus juice and bitters in a pisco sour cocktail, .

QUILQUIÑA

This herb is used in Bolivia and other South American countries to flavor salsas and soups. It is often substituted for cilantro, which has a similar taste. *Quilquiña* is found in Mexican and Latin markets.

QUINOA

Quinoa is an ancient grain with a flavor similar to barley. Before cooking quinoa, it must be rinsed in a fine-mesh sieve several times. After cooking, it has a creamy, slightly crunchy texture and nutty flavor. Quinoa can be found in many supermarkets; it is either black, white, or reddish in color.

SUGARCANE

Filled with sweetness, these stalks can be enjoyed as a snack, used as a swizzle stick for cocktails, or employed as a skewer for appetizers. The liquid from the stalks is processed into sugar, molasses, treacle, and rum. Sugarcane juice and stalks can be found at Latin or West Indian markets; the juice can be found at some supermarkets.

TAMARILLOS

Known as "tree tomatoes," this edible red-colored fruit is eaten raw throughout South America. They are much sweeter than tomatoes but have a hint of tartness. They can be used to make sweet and savory relishes. Tamarillos can be found at most supermarkets.

TARO

This tuber is used in many dishes, from soups to curries. The taste is dense and nutty, a bit sweeter than potatoes, but its texture is silky smooth. It can be sautéed or boiled and mashed like potatoes. Taro can be found at specialty markets or Latin and West Indian shops.

TOMATILLOS

A relative of the tomato, tomatillos also called "husk tomatoes." This green fruit has a papery husk that falls away easily; the waxy coating on the skin underneath should be rinsed off with warm water before using. Unlike tomatoes, tomatillos are very tart and are not eaten raw. Boiled and roasted, they are an essential ingredient in *salsa verde*. Tomatillos can be found at major supermarkets and at Latin and Mexican stores.

YERBA MATÉ

Yerba comes from the leaves and stems of a tree indigenous to South America. It is dried and crushed to make a tisane and sipped from a maté—a gourdlike container—through a *bombílla* (a straw used to filter the drink). Yerba tastes like a fusion of *matcha* green tea, woodsy roots, and dried old thyme. It's an acquired taste for some. This tisane can be found at specialty-foods markets.

YUCCA

This long tuber can be fried, boiled, or roasted. Sometimes called "cassava" or "manioc," yucca has a delicate but slightly bland taste. It can be substituted for boiled potatoes. Tapioca is made from yucca's starchy roots. Yucca can be found at Latin stores and supermarkets, usually next to the potatoes.

GEORGETOWN

GUYANA

TO PERU

I have visited rain forests around the world and the Iwokrama forest is one of the most pristine rain forests on the globe. It lies at the heart of the Guiana Shield, located in Guyana, and stretches into Venezuela, Brazil, and Suriname. Along with Amazonia, the Congo, and Papua New Guinea, the Guiana Shield is the last of its kind on this planet.

In 1989, Guyana donated more than one million acres of its virgin rain forest to the international community, creating the formal international identification of the Iwokrama Forest site. It's an oasis of biodiversity, science, conservation, and ecotourism; in reality, it's an experiment in sustainably managing a rain forest before it's destroyed.

The Iwokrama is home to some of the world's most endangered species, including the giant anteater, harpy eagle, jaguar, labria snake, giant river otter and turtle, black caiman, and the mighty anaconda. The thick, verdant forest canopy is a sanctuary for more than eight hundred species of birds, not to mention butterflies of various colors and shapes.

Guyana is an ecotourist's dream, with a wild interior riddled with rivers, mountains, wildlife, and waterfalls. Its slow pace, natural beauty, and low-profile tourism make it particularly appealing to me as I seek adventure off the beaten track.

Guyana's rivers teem with more than five hundred species of fish. I am familiar with some of them, including exotic beauties like the giant *arapaima*—at up to 10 feet long and 480 pounds, it is the world's largest scaled freshwater fish.

If you are an adventurous nocturnal creature like I am, you can glide down the mighty Essequibo River on a moonless night. You won't be alone; you'll see the shiny eyes of tree boas or night frogs, or the fire-red glare of the mighty black caiman, staring right back at you.

Mount Roraima, said to be the inspiration for Sir Arthur Conan Doyle's novel *The Lost World,* lies to the west, bordering Venezuela. The highest mountain in Guyana, Mount Roraima is one of the harshest places on the planet. Because it rains almost every day, life on this tabletop mountain is a fight for survival. It's also the home of carnivorous plants. East of Mount Roraima is the towering single-drop Kaieteur Falls, splashing down more than seven hundred feet.

As for the rest of the country, well, you can also stroll by Dutch architecture in the capital of Georgetown, or you can travel to the beaches of Berbice, where brown sugar–like sand and swaying palm trees await you.

This former British colony is the only English-speaking country in South America. Guyana gained its independence from the British in 1966 and is a melting pot of cuisines and cultures from around the world. You can find a mélange of food, as the country's extraordinary ethnic diversity makes for unparalleled, spicy cuisine and friendly, open-minded people from every corner of the planet. You can savor Portuguese, Indian, Chinese, African, and Amerindian meals at restaurants. Or, if you're lucky, someone will invite you to their home to break bread over fish or wild game soups, flavorful curries, noodles, or slow-simmered stews with ground provisions such as yucca, *eddoes* (taro), and plantains—and no Guyanese dish is complete without a steaming bowl of rice.

To see the heart and soul of this country, take a minibus ride to bustling outdoor markets throughout the coastal areas, small cities, and villages. There you will find farmers' markets teeming with the freshest ingredients from local farmers.

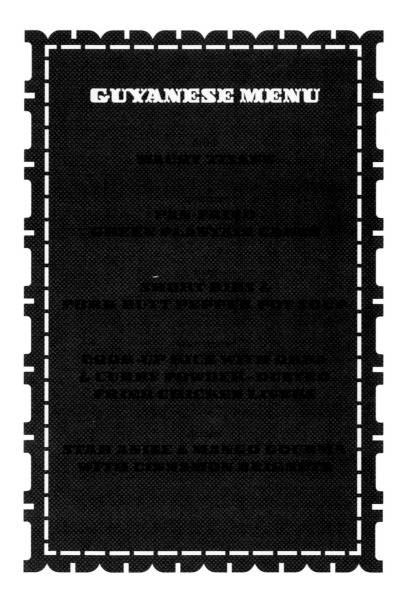

GUYANESE MENU

SHAUD CRABS

CRACKED
GREEN PLANTAIN CHIPS

SHORT RIBS &
PORK BUTT PEPPER POT SOUP

COOK-UP RICE WITH OKRO
& CURRY POWDER-DUSTED
FRIED CHICKEN LIVERS

STAR ANISE & MANGO COULINA
WITH CINNAMON BEIGNETS

At the beginning of December in many parts of South America, the equatorial rains begin. This downpour kept many villagers from coming to my childhood home in Guyana to seek help for their physical and spiritual ills. Instead, my grandfather Payo, an Ayurvedic doctor, Hindu priest, and family counselor, traveled from village to village to treat them. Our only means of transportation was a black Raleigh bicycle, which had no brakes. Payo would come to a full stop by touching his heel to the spinning back wheel.

One Saturday when I was six and a half, Payo and I traveled south toward the Amazon. It was the second time we visited Laxmi, one of Payo's patients. Along the way, we saw lazy smoke from kitchen pipes and smelled the morning aromas from the passing villages: kerosene, lit matches, wet firewood, curry simmering, and freshly cut grass.

Smoke streamed steadily out of Laxmi's kitchen. The wet mud floor squished through her tiny toes as she walked to the doorway to greet us. Payo acknowledged her with a nod and began to delve into his bag for her cures and his journal. Payo's soft brown cowhide medicine bag contained a variety of herbs, tonics, spices, a spice mortar and pestle, and a few journals with notes on everyone he treated.

Laxmi's stove was constructed of blue mud, rice straw, and cow dung. The fire in the mud stove was weak. On one of two burners always sat an old, dented one-gallon ghee tin. The Hindi script on the tin was barely visible from its soot-covered sides. In it she brewed the tea Payo had given her, made with *mauby* bark, plum cloves, and green cardamom pods. Laxmi strained the tea into two chipped yellow enamel cups. The beaten-up strainer trapped the long, cinnamon-like *mauby* bark, cloves, and cardamom. She sweetened the tea with brown demerara sugar.

The tea went down warm in my almost-empty morning stomach. The sweet smell of cloves and cardamom, and the tingly licorice taste of the *mauby* was delightful as it touched the back of my throat.

MAUBY TISANE

Throughout the West Indies, this drink, along with ginger beer, is the preferred homemade elixir. We practically lived on it. *Mauby* bark is an acquired taste, so you might have to adjust the sugar to your liking. I serve it in large punch bowls at picnics and at holiday parties. You will find *mauby* bark at West Indies and Latin markets.

20 cups water

2 green cardamon pods

6 large pieces *(about ½ oz)* *mauby* bark

Two 2-inch pieces cinnamon stick

1½ cups loosely packed brown sugar, plus more to taste

Ice

Orange slices for garnish

1. In a large stockpot over medium heat, combine 10 cups of the water, the cardamon, *mauby* bark, and cinnamon. Bring to a boil. Reduce the heat to low and simmer for 1½ hours.

2. Remove from the heat and cover. Let the mixture steep at room temperature for 2 hours or up to overnight.

3. A few hours before serving, add the remaining 10 cups of water and the 1½ cups of brown sugar.

4. Adjust the sweetness with more brown sugar as needed, and serve with lots of ice and garnish with a slice of orange.

PAN-FRIED GREEN PLANTAIN CAKES

These are a great after-school snack for children, or serve them as a side dish. The cakes can be made ahead and kept in a sealed container in the refrigerator for up to 2 days.

3 medium firm green plantains, peeled *(see note, page 101)* and cut into 1-inch pieces

Sea salt

1 Tbsp minced shallot

1 medium red jalapeño, seeded and finely chopped

1 tsp ground cumin

⅛ tsp ground turmeric

¼ cup fresh chopped cilantro

Freshly ground black pepper

3 Tbsp unsalted butter

1. In a large saucepan, combine plantains and 1 Tbsp of sea salt and add cold water to cover by 1 inch. Bring to a boil over medium heat and cook until tender, 10 to 15 minutes. Test for doneness by inserting a skewer into a plantain— it should go in easily.

2. Meanwhile, in a medium bowl, combine the shallot, jalapeño, cumin, turmeric, and cilantro.

3. When the plantains are done, drain and immediately transfer to a bowl with the shallot mixture. Toss lightly.

4. Using a masher, mash the plantains, mixing well. Season with salt and pepper. Allow to cool. Divide into 6 equal portions and form into smooth round patties.

5. In a 12-inch heavy skillet over medium heat, slowly heat the butter until it melts and becomes foamy. Pan-fry the plantains on both sides until nice and brown, about 5 minutes on each side.

6. Drain on a plate lined with paper towels and serve warm.

Hayari had a typical Arawak kitchen with a dirt floor. It was warm and cozy, and it smelled of burned cacao pods and coffee leaves. Several long poles with round rings at the end hung from the rough beams above. On the adjoining iron rods were S-hooks from which hung black cast-iron cauldrons. On the stove below—a round heap of a weak fire surrounded by stones—one open cauldron puffed a faint thread of steam.

The pantry shelf was lined with jars of salt and brown sugar. Next to them sat a Gilbey's gin bottle filled with brown caramelized *cassareep*. Hanging from the ceiling was a basket heaped with spices and dried herbs. Payo's Ayurvedic remedies were similar to those of the Arawak Indians. Their shamans also used natural herbs, spices, barks, and leaves from the Amazon to cure their ailments.

Hayari handed me a bowl of ripe sedums, which look like red seedless grapes, except that they do have three small, hard seeds. The flesh of the sedum is sweet with a tinge of tartness and tastes similar to red plums. I sat in the hammock feasting on sedums as I sighted a dead guinea fowl in a plastic bowl by the table outside the kitchen. Its neck still dangled on a piece of its skin, and a few flies feasted on the severed bone. I spat the sedum seeds into the small puddle of water by the hammock, and a few chickens rushed to pick at them.

Then Hayari handed me the bowl with the guinea fowl. I took half of a dried coconut and turned it over onto the dirt floor, sitting on the smooth side. I had seen Hayari make pepper pot many times, but this was the first time we used guinea fowl. Previously, we had used pig tails, oxtails, venison, ducks, ham hocks, pig's ears, totters, and goat tripe. Hayari's cooking was limited to variations of this one dish, just like Laxmi's different versions of cook-up.

Pepper pot was invented by the Arawak Indians, and even the slaves from Africa whom the Dutch and British brought to Guyana cooked the same way. They learned to prepare one-pot meals by collecting the scraps their masters threw out, so everything edible ended up in one pot. Pepper pot is the treasure of all Guyanese soups and stews; sometimes it is used as a main meal.

Hayari carefully poured the boiling water from the cauldron onto the fowl. This helped loosen the feathers as I began to pluck the bird, exposing its pimply olive-colored skin. Hayari returned the empty cauldron to the stove and added fresh rainwater to boil. Then he took down the hanging basket and picked out bay leaves, allspice berries, cloves, one whole habanero chile, and some dried thyme, and added them to the pot. I took his machete and his mango-wood chopping block and began to slice, then chop, the defeathered fowl.

Hayari poured the thick *cassareep* from the gin bottle into the cauldron. The pepper pot simmered as Hayari added several more dried coconut shells to set the fire ablaze. I rinsed the chopped pieces of fowl with water gushing from one of his gutters. I handed the bowl to him, and he added it to the bubbling cauldron and covered it. I rinsed my hands again and we both began to shell black-eyed peas. We ate most of them as we watched the flames dancing on the zinc kitchen walls.

SHORT RIBS & PORK BUTT PEPPER POT SOUP

{ serves 6 to 8 }

This soup has been savored by the natives of Guyana for hundreds of years. The Arawak Indians made this one-pot meal with lots of chiles indigenous to South America. Newcomers from Africa and India have contributed to this dish throughout the years. The main ingredient that makes it a pepper pot is the condiment *cassareep,* found at West Indian supermarkets; if you can't find it, blackstrap molasses can be substituted. Serve pepper pot as a main meal with rice or potatoes, or spoon it over your favorite cooked pasta.

3 Tbsp extra-virgin olive oil

1 lb beef short ribs, cut into 2-inch pieces

1½ lb pork butt, cut into 2-inch pieces

2 large red onions, finely chopped

2 Tbsp minced garlic

One 4-inch piece fresh ginger, peeled and finely chopped

1 Tbsp finely chopped fresh thyme

Two 3-inch pieces cinnamon stick

Sea salt

¾ cup *cassareep* or ½ cup blackstrap molasses

6 cups low-sodium beef or vegetable stock

1 whole habanero chile, stem on *(optional)* or 1 Tbsp crushed red chile flakes

Freshly ground black pepper

In a large stockpot, heat the olive oil over high heat. Working in batches, brown the short ribs and pork butt.

Remove the meat from the pot, reduce the heat to low, and add the onions, garlic, ginger, thyme, cinnamon sticks, and 2 tsp salt. Stir until the onions are soft, about 3 minutes. Add the *cassareep,* and cook stirring frequently, for 1 minute more.

Return the meats to the pot and the add the stock. Bring to a boil, cover, and reduce the heat to a slow simmer. Cook until the meat is falling off the bones, about 2 hours.

About 15 minutes before the dish is finished, add the whole habanero chile or crushed red pepper flakes (if using).

Season with salt and pepper. Serve warm.

As we ventured on bicycle to Laxmi's house that morning when I was a child, a soft drizzle of rain coated the vendant, green grass. The mist sent the tiny hairs on my arms into hundreds of pimply chicken bumps. Blue tarps dotted the villages, cocooning many of the gray plank houses, but little did they help. Some homes collapsed or floated away. The equatorial rains lashed at everything in sight, and people became prisoners in their homes.

Laxmi's small front yard had several rows of lush, tall trees bearing long okra pods. Several black-and-yellow bumblebees hovered around the okra trees' yellow flowers, which looked like hibiscus. The roof of Laxmi's chicken coop was home to her three boney Creole fowls. They clucked and picked at leftover grated coconut in brown half-shells. Some Muscovy ducks swam excitedly and quacked in the flooded trenches next to her house.

In Laxmi's kitchen, next to the ghee tin, a badly chipped blue enamel pot contained my favorite one-pot meal: "cook-up." She had begun preparing it at 3 AM, and it had been sitting there for hours. Laxmi knew how to cook only one meal, and that was cook-up.

During the rainy season, many villagers, at least the poor ones, cooked only one meal a day because all their dry firewood would otherwise become wet or damp. They could not keep it inside their houses since snakes, centipedes, and scorpions would crawl into the wood piles to seek refuge from the rain.

Cook-up is poor man's food. When there isn't much food available, villagers take whatever is lying around and cook it all in one pot. Rice and coconut milk are always the main ingredients. If you are fortunate, then you can add shrimp, chicken, beef, pork, or salted or smoked fish.

I took small spoonfuls of lukewarm cook-up into my mouth. The soft-boiled rice with long pieces of whole green okra, plump black-eyed peas, and coconut milk felt hearty and comforting. The large pieces of okra were silky on my tongue.

Laxmi was the skinniest woman I ever saw. She smelled of Bengay, limes, and coconut oil. Payo told me that few people visited her. They called her *pagli* (crazy) and gossiped about her. She was seventeen and had gotten married when she was thirteen, but she looked like she was older than my mother. She walked with a limp. She claimed she had broken her ankle last summer fetching a large burlap bag of coconut shells to kindle her fire.

Her drunken husband would curse at her and complain that his arranged marriage was to a barren woman. He did not want to have "relations" with her but wanted her to have children. According to Payo's journals, there were times when Laxmi's husband dragged her by the hair into the kitchen and pelted her with the hot cook-up she had prepared for him just because she didn't add chicken. These entries were often followed by an Ayurvedic recipe of spices and herbs for the cure for this abuse.

While working on the fire in her kitchen, Laxmi unleashed the sorrowful words from her trapped heart about the torture from her husband. Payo took pencil to journal like a secretary; as he listened, he handed me pinches of herbs and spices from his bag. I slowly crushed the spices using the mini masala brick to make a tea remedy for her drunken husband.

I welcomed the warm aroma of the crushed spices and wondered if Laxmi loved her husband. Was there magic in these spices powerful enough to take away the abuse she experienced and bring her peace? Payo had been teaching me that if you talk to the spices they will listen, healing us or making the food taste better, even if you are not a good cook.

After leaving Laxmi's village, we rode silently to another patient. The coconut trees bordering the pitch road swayed from side to side against the Amazon wind. It was drizzling. With the aftertaste of licorice from the *mauby* tea in my mouth, I prayed that Laxmi could cook another dish and that her husband would not abuse her again.

COOK-UP RICE WITH OKRA & CURRY POWDER–DUSTED FRIED CHICKEN LIVERS

This is the ultimate comfort food for all Guyanese. Every cook makes their own version, varying the meat. I like mine topped off with fried chicken, fish, or, my all-time favorite, curry-crusted crispy liver. In my home these spiced livers are also served with mashed potatoes or on top of pasta or plain white rice. The cook-up rice can also be served as a side dish with steaks or pork chops.

1 cup dried black-eyed peas, soaked for about 4 hours

⅓ cup extra-virgin olive oil

1 large red onion, finely chopped

2 Tbsp minced garlic

1 tsp finely chopped fresh oregano

1 tsp finely chopped fresh thyme

Sea salt

4½ cups low-sodium chicken stock

1 cup parboiled rice

1 cup canned unsweetened coconut milk

1 whole habanero chile (*optional*)

6 small whole baby okras, stemmed

2 Tbsp sliced green onion (*green part only*)

Freshly ground black pepper

Curry Powder–Dusted Fried Chicken Livers for serving (*facing page*)

1. Drain the black-eyed peas and set aside.

2. Heat the olive oil over medium-high heat in a large pot. Add the onion, garlic, oregano, thyme and 1 tsp salt and cook until the onion is softened, about 2 minutes.

3. Add the stock and drained peas and bring to a boil. Reduce the heat to medium and cook, uncovered, until the peas are nearly tender, about 15 minutes.

4. Reduce the heat to low and add the rice, coconut milk, and habanero (if using). Simmer, covered, for 20 minutes more, stirring occasionally.

5. Turn off the heat, and add the whole okra's and green onion, and let cook-up steam in the pot, lid on, for 5 minutes more. Season with salt and pepper. Serve warm with the fried chicken livers.

CURRY POWDER–DUSTED FRIED CHICKEN LIVERS

{ serves 6 to 8 }

Vegetable oil for deep-frying

1 Tbsp curry powder

1 tsp garlic powder

1 tsp cayenne pepper

¼ cup all-purpose flour

1½ lb chicken livers

Sea salt

Freshly ground black pepper

1. In a heavy skillet over medium heat, slowly heat enough oil for deep-frying (about 3 inches) until a deep-fry thermometer reads 365°F.

2. On a large plate, combine the curry powder, garlic powder, cayenne, and flour and mix well. Dredge the livers one piece at a time, in the flour and shake off excess.

3. Place the livers into the pan and fry until cooked through and crisp, about 1 to 2 minutes on each side. Only turn once and don't overcook them, or they'll turn out chewy and bitter.

4. Drain the livers on paper towels. Sprinkle with salt and pepper. Serve warm.

Butcher Mangal lived in a large, white-painted concrete house; it was also a grocery store and a rum shop. A symbol of wealth, it stood majestically on stilts in a lonely village. His house overlooked the vast, open savannah to the west. Butcher Mangal had a great reputation for his black pudding. He learned how to clean the innards of the pig properly and what spices were important before he earned his credentials for the tastiest black pudding in the region.

The kitchen was a separate structure at the back of the house. Its floors were made of concrete and then layered with polished purple heartwood from the Amazon rain forest. There was a sink and a pipe, but no running water. Instead, there was a yellow plastic bucket filled with rainwater. A square white freezer looked and opened like a squeaking coffin. It operated with electricity produced by a generator, another symbol of wealth. There were no wood-burning fires or mud stoves but rather four green one-burner kerosene stoves. All the burners were lit. The deep-red flames heated the pots that were bubbling steam or smoking oil.

The kitchen exuded the layered aroma of cooked cream and crushed nutmeg married with roasted spices from a garam masala blend. There was a lingering hint of boiled blood, pounded garlic, steamed meats, and ripe star fruit. Then, it intensified to another layer as the steam drew to my nostrils a woodsy but floral bouquet from crushed broad-leaf oregano. It was a clean kitchen. I wanted to spend the rest of my life in it.

Radha, the maid, brought me a large glass of warm cow's milk with froth on top. I let it sit and watched as the thick layer of clotted cream developed. I scooped it up with my yellow, turmeric-stained finger. It hung lusciously wet and tasted rich and sweet. Radha placed a saucer with a piece of perfectly thick, square milk fudge and stewed mangoes with decadent spices in front of me. She made milk fudge and mango *gourma* all the time because Butcher Mangal and his wife had lots of cow's milk.

Radha's fudge was known in several villages. She added an ingredient Payo told her to use: nutmeg. He told her she needed to chew on pieces of it to help balance her talkative ways. So Radha added nutmeg to all the dishes she loved. She even grated it into the mango *gourma*, which was not supposed to have nutmeg, just star anise and vanilla. Her mango *gourma* recipe called for the hard seeds of the mango to be simmered with the flesh for hours. Then you would suck up all the warm, sugary juices and chew on the seeds for the rest of the day; it was one of my favorite childhood recipes.

In the fudge recipe, she did not grate the nutmeg but instead pounded it into tiny pieces the size of coffee grounds and added a handful of freshly grated coconut, fresh cow's milk, and brown sugar. When you bit into the fudge, the sweet milk coated the tiny pieces of sweet nutmeg, which burst into your mouth as if drinking chai.

Her best fudge was when she used the "first milk." After the heifer gives birth to the calf, the milk that comes out first is thick and clotted like cream and is the sweetest thing you will ever taste.

Radha called me to the stove, and I guzzled the last of my warm milk, wiping the drips on my chin with the back of my hands. I packed the remaining fudge and mango into my mouth, chewing quickly. She handed me a link of the crispy, glossy black pudding. I tossed it between my palms to cool. The boiled blood and warm pieces of meat started to make my mouth water. I gulped down the sugary fudge-and-mango liquid before I carefully nibbled the crispy, hot black pudding casing. I broke the brittle skin with my teeth and the insides flaked onto my tongue and fell into my palm. I picked up the soft, spice-crusted pieces of offal and boiled blood with my lips. I did not have to move my jaw; the pudding just melted on my tongue.

STAR ANISE & MANGO GOURMA WITH CINNAMON BEIGNETS

{ serves 6 to 8 }

Gourma is a dish made at Hindu religious functions and served with the puffy fried wheat cakes called *pooris*. Every home in Guyana has a unique version, as does mine in New York. I like to serve *gourma* with beignets, since they make it less messy to savor this beloved sweet treat. I stuff the extra beignets with fresh fruits or eggs and bacon for breakfast or with salads at lunchtime. You can also skip the beignets and enjoy these mangoes with a scoop of your favorite ice cream.

4 large mangoes, peeled and sliced

1 cup sugar

One 2-inch piece cinnamon stick

3 star anise

1 vanilla bean, halved lengthwise, seeds scraped out and bean reserved

Cinnamon Beignets for serving *(facing page)*

1. In a medium heavy-bottomed saucepan, combine the mangoes with enough water to cover by 1 inch.

2. Add the sugar, cinnamon, star anise, vanilla seeds, and vanilla bean. Cover and simmer over medium heat until the mangoes are soft and have turned golden yellowish, about 10 to 12 minutes. Remove from the heat and allow to cool. Discard the star anise and vanilla bean.

3. Slice the rectangle-shaped beignets in half lengthwise, making a pocket. Take 1 or 2 slices of the mango gourma and place it between each sliced beignet to serve.

{ makes 8 beignets }

CINNAMON BEIGNETS

2¼ cups all-purpose flour,
plus more for dusting

1 Tbsp baking powder

1 tsp ground cinnamon

1 tsp sea salt

1 stick (½ *cup*) unsalted
butter, melted

2 Tbsp sugar

Vegetable oil for frying

1 In a large mixing bowl, sift together the 2¼ cups flour, baking powder, cinnamon, and salt. Add the melted butter and sugar and mix with a fork until the butter is well combined.

2 Slowly add about ½ cup water, then gently knead the dough until it forms a ball. Do not add too much water at a time or the dough will become too sticky. Continue to knead for 3 minutes more until the dough becomes slightly elastic.

3 Pat the dough into a rectangle on a lightly floured surface. Roll out to ¼-inch thickness, adding more flour if necessary. Cover with a damp towel and let rest for 10 minutes.

4 In a heavy skillet over medium heat, slowly heat enough oil for deep-frying (about 3 inches) until a deep-fry thermometer reads 365°F.

5 Cut the dough into eight 6-by-3-inch rectangles. Drop the dough pieces into hot oil and fry in small batches, turning when they are just golden, about 2 minutes on each side. When both sides are golden brown, remove the beignets with a slotted spoon and transfer to a plate lined with paper towels. Allow to cool.

TO SURINAME

FROM GUYANA

IQUITOS

PE
RU

LIMA

CUZCO

Peru's enigma of a landscape stretches from the Amazon across the Andes to the Pacific Coast. I wandered through the incomparable ancient mountain city of Machu Picchu, lost myself in the maze of the bustling former Incan capital, Cuzco, and reflected in awe about the magnitude of the mysterious Nazca Lines. Peru, the land of the Incas where food is sacred, has one of the most impeccable and intact cultures I have ever experienced.

The culinary history of Peruvian food dates back to the Incas and pre-Incas with ingredients we Americans are all too familiar with, such as *maize* (corn) and *papas* (potatoes). Typical Peruvian dishes are tasty and vary regionally. There is a wide variety of vegetables, especially potatoes. Of the five thousand varieties of *papas* available worldwide, there are more than two thousand kinds found in Peru alone, each with a unique shape and color. Potatoes have been cultivated in Peru for an estimated six thousand years in the high-altitude areas of the Andes. In every city or village market I frequented, I was amazed at the variety of potatoes: from every color imaginable to some as small as almonds to long and twisted ones. One of my favorite potato dishes from Peru is *ají de gallina,* a spicy chicken dish with cashews, *ají* (chiles), and potatoes.

Peru's coastline and vast lakes, surrounded by verdant farms, bring about an abundance of markets teeming with a variety of fresh ingredients that can sate any appetite. In the coastal regions, seafood is understandably the best choice. Peru's popular seafood dish is ceviche, a raw-fish appetizer marinated in lime or lemon juice along with chiles, red onions, and cilantro. Another well-loved meal is my favorite soup, *chupe de camarones* (shrimp soup).

In the Andes and Amazon highlands I discovered perhaps one of the most adventurous meals I've tasted, via an unusual cooking technique called *pachamanca.* The term comes from the Quechua word *pacha mama* (Mother Earth). *Pachamanca* involves an underground oven where the food is cooked for a few hours using fire-heated stones and banana leaves between layers of the ingredients. A range of meats are typical, such as *cuy* (guinea pig), llama, or alpaca, together with potatoes, beans, and *ají.* The meat is covered with aromatic *marmaquilla* (an indigenous herb) leaves. This method of cooking was a special spiritual ritual for the Incas, who worshipped Mother Earth. *Pachamanca* symbolizes food from her womb and is performed to honor her and give thanks to the fertility of the land for future crops.

Another essential ingredient in the Peruvian pantry is corn, which is used in rituals and provided sustenance for the Incas for hundreds of years. It is abundant and there are many varieties, including plump white, yellow, and purple; some have kernels as big as quarters. Peanuts, *ají,* and quinoa, the wonder food of the Incan diet, complete the cuisine here.

PERUVIAN MENU

drink
GUAVA PISCO SOUR

soup
CHUPE DE CAMARONES
shrimp soup

salad
PAPAS A LA HUANCAÍNA
peruvian potato salad

appetizer
ANTICUCHOS
peruvian skewered beef tenderloin

main course
QUINOA TURKEY MEATLOAF

dessert
PICARONES
sweet potato donuts

GUAVA PISCO SOUR

{ serves 2 }

The Mexicans have tequila, the Russians have vodka, and the Peruvians have pisco, thanks to vines brought from the Canary Islands in the mid-1500s. The pisco sour is the national cocktail, likely concocted in Lima. In this version, I've added guava juice, but your favorite juice will also do.

½ cup pisco

½ cup canned or bottled guava nectar or juice

1 tsp superfine sugar

2 Tbsp freshly squeezed lime juice

A few dashes of Angostura bitters

Crushed ice

Fresh mint for garnish

Lime wedges for garnish

1 In a medium glass pitcher, combine the pisco, guava nectar, sugar, and lime juice with the bitters, and stir well to dissolve the sugar.

2 Divide the mixture between 2 glasses. Add the crushed ice.

3 Garnish each glass with fresh mint and a lime wedge to serve.

Now, if there is a beverage—and an alcoholic one, I may add—that is good enough to have an entire day devoted to it, then I am there to see what's so special about it. On February 8, I hitched a ride on the back of a 4x4 on the Pan-American Highway to the Arequipa valley. It was National Pisco Sour Day in Peru. The distilleries were packed with locals who wanted to be merry. They were drinking Acholado (or Creole) pisco, which is distilled from a variety of aromatic and nonaromatic grapes. They believe this type of pisco to be the best—and I agreed. The others I tasted were pure pisco, made from grape varieties such as mollar, common black, and quebranta; aromatic pisco, made from Italia, Torrentes, or muscat grapes; and *mosto verde*, which is distilled from unfermented grape juice.

As I sipped away, I was told by the locals how the national drink got its name from the Peruvian port where it is rumored to have been created. As one man spoke, the others listened quietly, but their faces were gleaming with pride about their national drink.

CHUPE DE CAMARONES

shrimp soup

On my way to Lima from Arequipa, I stopped in a beautiful town called Camaná, where I first sampled this divine soup. Camaná is situated on the coast, and its backyard is an agricultural oasis of verdant valleys and rivers teeming with *camarones* (shrimp). After numerous attempts to replicate this soup at home, I found that the perfect texture could be achieved only with russet potatoes. It truly took me back to that first spoonful in Camaná. Serve with plaintain chips (page 101), if you like.

2 Tbsp extra-virgin olive oil

1 small onion, finely chopped

1 Tbsp minced garlic

Sea salt

1 Tbsp sweet paprika

½ tsp cayenne pepper

1 tsp ground annatto

2 cups peeled and diced russet potatoes *(about 2 large or 3 medium potatoes)*

6 cups low-sodium fish or vegetable stock

1 lb large shrimp, peeled and deveined, tails left on if desired

1 cup canned or frozen whole corn kernels

Freshly ground black pepper

¼ cup fresh cilantro sprigs

1. In a large saucepan, heat the olive oil over medium heat. Add the onion, garlic, and a pinch of salt. Sauté until soft, stirring frequently, about 2 to 3 minutes. Add the paprika, cayenne, and annatto and cook for 3 minutes more, stirring frequently.

2. Add the potatoes and stir until coated with mixture. Add the stock and bring to a boil. Reduce the heat to low and cover. Simmer until the potatoes are fork-tender, 20 to 25 minutes. Add the shrimp and corn and cook for 5 minutes more.

3. Season with salt and pepper. Add the cilantro and stir. Remove from the heat and ladle into soup bowls. Serve hot.

PAPAS A LA HUANCAÍNA

{ serves 4 to 6 }

peruvian potato salad

This salad was my savior while climbing the trail up to Machu Picchu. *Papas a la huancaína* is a Peruvian salad of potatoes covered in a *huancaína* sauce, named after Huancayo, a city located in the lush Mantaro River Valley. The delicious creamy sauce is made with coconut milk, cheese, and *ají amaríllo* (yellow chili powder) and served with hard-boiled eggs. The salad gives new meaning to the notion of potato salad.

2 lb russet potatoes, peeled and cut into ½-inch dice

Sea salt

2 Tbsp extra-virgin olive oil

1 tsp minced garlic

1 small shallot, minced

1 Tbsp *ají amarillo* powder or sweet paprika powder

One 14-oz can unsweetened coconut milk

6 oz shredded Monterey Jack cheese

½ cup chopped fresh cilantro

Freshly ground black pepper

4 large hard-boiled eggs, peeled and coarsely chopped

In a large saucepan, combine the potatoes and 1 tsp salt and add enough cold water to cover by 1 inch. Bring to a boil over medium heat. Cover and cook until the potatoes are just tender but still firm, 8 to 10 minutes. Immediately drain and set aside to cool, or refrigerate until ready to use.

Meanwhile, in a medium nonstick saucepan, heat the olive oil over low heat. Sauté the garlic, shallot, and *ají amarillo* powder for 2 minutes, or until the mixture is soft. Whisk in the coconut milk and cheese, and continue to whisk constantly until the mixture is reduced to about ¾ cup. Add the cilantro and whisk for another minute. Season with salt and pepper.

In a large bowl, place the boiled potatoes. Pour in the cheese mixture. Mix well until all the potatoes are coated. Transfer to a serving bowl and sprinkle with the eggs before serving. Serve immediately or cover with plastic wrap and refrigerate until ready to serve.

MAKE-AHEAD TIP The sauce and cooked potatoes can be made a day ahead and stored separately, covered, in the refrigerator until ready to use.

ANTICUCHOS

peruvian skewered beef tenderloin

Anticuchos, a Quechua word for kebabs, are found in any Peruvian city and sold by street-food vendors. They are made from small pieces of grilled meat that have been marinated in spices. The preferred meat in Peru is beef or goat heart, but I use beef tenderloin because it's easily available.

1 lb beef tenderloin, cut into 1-inch cubes

1 small ear fresh corn, husks and silks removed, cut into 4 equal pieces

8 small whole cooked red bliss potatoes *(see note)*

4 Tbsp extra-virgin olive oil

4 Tbsp red wine vinegar

2 tsp *ají amarillo* chile powder or paprika powder

½ tsp minced garlic

½ tsp ground cumin

½ tsp crushed dried thyme

Sea salt

Freshly ground black pepper

Lime wedges for garnish

1 Divide the beef equally and thread the cubes onto four 10-to-12 inch metal skewers, alternating with one piece of corn and two potatoes on each skewer. Place the *anticuchos* in a large baking pan.

2 In a small bowl, whisk togther the olive oil, vinegar, *ají amarillo* powder, garlic, cumin, and thyme. Rub the marinade on *anticuchos* to coat, cover with plastic wrap, and refrigerate for 1 to 2 hours or up to overnight.

3 Build a hot fire in a charcoal grill or heat a gas grill until very hot. Grill *anticuchos* until medium-rare, 3 to 5 minutes on each side, or longer for well done.

4 Transfer the *anticuchos* to a serving platter and sprinkle with salt and pepper. Serve warm with the lime wedges.

NOTES In a small saucepan, combine potatoes and a pinch of salt. Cover with cold water by 1 inch. Bring to a boil over medium heat, cover, and cook until potatoes are just tender but still firm, about 5 minutes. Immediately drain and set aside to cool.

The *anticuchos* can also be cooked in a preheated broiler following the same directions above.

QUINOA TURKEY MEATLOAF {serves 6 to 8}

In the Andean city of Cuzco, I watched as the street vendors prepared *humitas*, yellow-corn tamales wrapped in corn husks and steamed the same way Mexican tamales are made. As the vendor quickly formed smooth mounds of the cornmeal, I couldn't help but think of how I would mold meatloaf. Then I remembered the main ingredient from my meal the previous night: quinoa. I decided to marry the two in this signature dish. It's full of protein and absolutely delicious—the perfect alternative to the same old meatloaf.

2 Tbsp extra-virgin olive oil

1 large onion, finely chopped

1 medium jalapeño, seeded and finely chopped

1 Tbsp ground cumin

1½ cups cooked quinoa (*see note*)

1 lb ground turkey

¼ cup chopped fresh basil

¼ cup chopped fresh chives

2 Tbsp tomato paste

1 large egg, lightly beaten

1 tsp sea salt

1 tsp freshly ground black pepper

1 Preheat the oven to 375°F. Grease an 8½-by-4½-by-2½-inch glass loaf pan.

2 In a heavy skillet, heat the olive oil over medium heat. Add the onion and jalapeño and sauté until soft, about 5 minutes. Add the cumin and cook for 1 minute more. Transfer to a large bowl.

3 Add the cooked quinoa, turkey, basil, chives, tomato paste, egg, salt, and pepper to bowl and mix thoroughly.

4 Transfer to the prepared loaf pan. Bake for 1 hour, turn oven off, and let the meatloaf rest for 10 minutes more. Remove from oven and let cool for 5 minutes. Slice and serve.

NOTE To make the quinoa, place ½ cup dried quinoa in a fine-mesh sieve; rinse and drain well. In a medium saucepan, combine the drained quinoa and 1 cup water or any type of stock. Bring to a boil over high heat. Reduce the heat to a simmer, cover, and cook until all of the water is absorbed, about 15 minutes. The quinoa is done when all the grains have turned from white to translucent and the spiral-like germ of the grain is visible. This portion yields 1½ cups cooked quinoa. The quinoa can be cooked a day ahead and stored, covered, in the refrigerator until ready to use.

After a day of pisco sour drinking, my head felt like a speeding train with no destination. My driver, Miguel, brought forth a shot glass with a murky-looking liquid that he called "Peruvian Viagra," aka *jugo blanco* (white juice) or *leche de tigre* (tiger's milk), to help cure me. I insisted that I had a hangover, but he said it would cure that, too. I rolled my eyes, and the way I was feeling, I think they kept on rolling.

His concoction consisted of the leftover marinade of lime juice from the raw-seafood dish ceviche. His mother, Isabelle, however, rescued me in the nick of time. She sat me down next to her wood-burning stove and brought forth a plate with a mound of donuts. Donuts aren't usually my thing, but I couldn't stop eating. I must have had about six!

PICARONES

{ makes 6 picarones }

sweet potato donuts

These doughy delights are made with sweet potatoes, and local cooks drizzle them with sugary syrup. I've tweaked the recipe to my own tastes, though, by topping them here with honey and superfine sugar.

1 medium unpeeled sweet potato *(about 12 oz)*, **scrubbed**

⅓ cup all-purpose flour, plus more for dusting

½ tsp baking powder

⅛ tsp ground cinnamon

⅛ tsp freshly grated nutmeg

Vegetable oil for deep-frying

Honey for drizzling

Superfine sugar for dusting

1 Place the potato with skin in a large saucepan. Add enough cold water to cover by 1 inch, bring to a boil over medium heat, and cook for about 40 minutes. Test for doneness by inserting a fork into the potato—it should slide off the fork easily. Drain the potato and transfer to a medium bowl to cool. When cool enough to handle, peel and force through a ricer. Discard any tough fibers. You should have about 1½ cups of mashed sweet potato.

2 In a medium mixing bowl, sift together flour, baking powder, cinnamon, and nutmeg. Add the mashed potatoes, kneading lightly until smooth. Form into a round ball. Break off small pieces of dough so you have six pieces, about 4 tablespoons each. Flour your hands lightly to prevent the dough from breaking and then roll the pieces of dough into smooth balls.

3 Flatten the balls slightly and make a hole through the center of each with your finger or the floured handle of a wooden spoon. Hold the dough in your palm and carefully smooth the edges around the hole with your fingers. Repeat until all the dough is shaped. Lay the donuts on a lightly floured tray.

4 In a heavy skillet over high heat, slowly heat enough oil for deep-frying (about 3 inches) until a deep-fry thermometer reads 365°F. Fry one donut at a time until golden brown, about 15 seconds on each side. Drain on a plate lined with paper towels.

5 Drizzle the donuts with the honey and dust with the sugar. Serve warm.

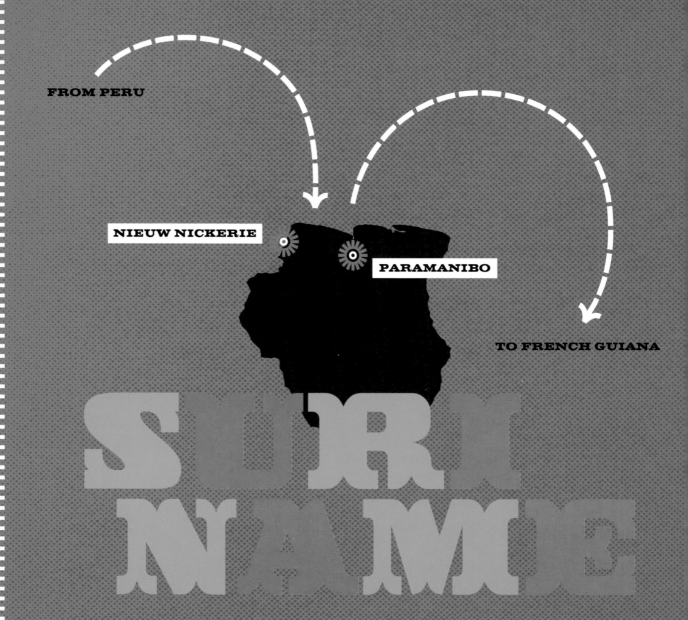

FROM PERU

NIEUW NICKERIE

PARAMANIBO

TO FRENCH GUIANA

SURI NAME

One of the smallest independent countries in South America, Suriname is tucked away at the northeastern tip of the continent between Guyana and French Guiana. In the seventeenth century, the Dutch traded New Amsterdam, now New York, with the British for Suriname. It remained a territory governed by the Netherlands until 1975, when it gained its independence.

Suriname is ethnically diverse, with its indigenous Amerindians, the Arawak; Caribs; and Africans, whom the Dutch brought over as slaves. Indians from India, Javanese from Indonesia, and Chinese from China came as indentured servants in the late 1800s. Newcomers adding color to the landscape included Brazilians, many of whom were of Portuguese descent and who came as gold miners.

Suriname's official language is Dutch, although each ethnic group speaks its own language. But what everyone has in common is a unique language that rolls off the tongue. *Taki-Taki* (or Sranan) is a fusion of Creole-English derived from the Maroons, who were descendants of runaway slaves.

There are a few sublime English words I can use to describe Suriname: untouched, primitive, and mysterious. Here, nature is as diverse as the country's ethnic cultures. About 80 percent of Suriname is covered by the rain forest's thick, impenetrable fortress of trees reaching toward the azure sky.

The funnest way to chart your adventure is to follow the many snakelike rivers that lead to several nature reserves and national parks. A splendor of raw beauty awaits your eyes. Monkeys, birds, and sea turtles call Suriname their domain, and if you are a botanist, then paradise is found with the sight of rare, exotic orchids. To cool off in this hot, humid climate, you have the option of taking a refreshing dip in waterfalls, wild rapids, or untouched ocean beaches.

In the cities of Nieuw Nickerie and Paramaribo (or Parbo), you will find white-washed wooden houses with rusty zinc roofs. Vines of lovely hot-pink bougainvillea hang on verandas and shutters. Chinese casinos flashing neon signs, shiny minaret-topped mosques, Hindu temples, Christian churches, and a Jewish synagogue also dot the landscape.

As for food, just follow the aroma into the many ethnic neighborhoods and you will find a mélange of delicacies. Examples include African-type dishes such as *tom-tom,* a peanut soup with plantain-flour noodles; another favorite is *heri heri,* which is made with boiled yucca, plantains, sweet potatoes, and *eddoes* and topped with salted and smoked fish. Hot-pepper sauce made with limes and habanero chiles is indispensable on every kitchen table and street-food cart. Native Amerindian cereals such as *kwak,* made from dried yucca, are simply delicious with coconut milk. Samosas, mango *lassi,* roti, and duck curry along with *gulab jammu* make up the Indian menu. Javanese *saoto,* a chicken soup with thinly sliced celery and taro and topped with a hard-boiled egg, is a delight to the palate. In Brazilian neighborhoods, you will find a wealth of Portuguese foods, from Nova Schin beer and *guarana* and Sumol drinks to beans, pasta, and delicious homemade *linguiça* (sausage).

An abundance of fresh fruits and vegetables makes up the Suriname food basket. It includes cherries, sometimes called "West Indian cherries," mangoes, papayas, soursop, jackfruit, plantains, star fruit, passion fruit, rambutans, black-eyed and pigeon peas, okra, eggplant, sweet potatoes, long beans, and bitter melons. The endless shorelines and rivers teem with fish, crab, and shrimp. To cool down your thirst on hot and humid days, there is nothing like flagging down the ice-man for a scoop of shaved ice topped with a rainbow array of your choice of flavored syrups.

SURINAMESE MENU

drink
FEIJOA PINEAPPLE PUNCH

soup
JAVANESE SOTO AYAM
coconut milk & shrimp soup

appetizer
AFRICAN-STYLE BAKED COO-COO
stuffed okra with shrimp

main course
INDONESIAN BAMI GORENG
stir-fry noodles with chicken

dessert
COCONUT-RASPBERRY BREAD & BUTTER PUDDING

FEIJOA PINEAPPLE PUNCH {serves 2}

If you cannot find feijoa (see page 16), then use guava or pineapple juice. I prefer this punch with rum, but the liquor can be omitted for a refreshing virgin cocktail.

¾ cup feijoa or guava juice

¼ cup dark rum

½ cup crushed pineapple

1½ cups crushed ice

2 feijoa or pineapple wedges for garnish

1 Pour the feijoa juice, rum, pineapple, and ice into a blender and blend until smooth. Divide between 2 hurricane glasses.

2 Garnish each drink with a feijoa wedge and serve.

JAVANESE SOTO AYAM

{ serves 6 }

coconut milk & shrimp soup

This is a delightful and warming soup. It might appear complicated, but it truly is not. And it cooks in less than half an hour.

¼ cup extra-virgin olive oil

1 small shallot, minced

1 Tbsp minced garlic

1 cup shredded white or Chinese cabbage

Sea salt

3 Tbsp curry powder

4 cups low-sodium chicken stock

3 cups canned unsweetened coconut milk

1½ lb large shrimp, peeled and deveined, thawed if frozen

½ lb dried rice-stick noodles or rice vermicelli

¼ cup freshly squeezed lime juice

Freshly ground black pepper

¼ cup chopped fresh cilantro

3 hard-boiled eggs, peeled and halved

1 lime, cut into 6 wedges, for garnish

1. In a large saucepan, heat the olive oil over medium heat. Add the shallot, garlic, cabbage, and a pinch of salt. Cook, stirring, until the cabbage is softened. Add the curry powder and cook, stirring, for 2 minutes more. Add the stock and coconut milk. Bring to a boil.

2. Reduce the heat to low, add the shrimp, and simmer until shrimp are opaque throughout, 8 to 10 minutes.

3. Meanwhile, in a medium pot of boiling salted water, cook the noodles until just tender but still firm to bite, about 6 minutes. Drain; rinse under cold water to cool.

4. Add the lime juice and season the soup with salt and pepper. Divide the noodles among 6 bowls. Ladle the hot soup into bowls. Sprinkle each with the cilantro and garnish with a hard-boiled egg half and a lime wedge. Serve hot.

63

Payo and Mayo (my grandfather and grandmother), Uncle Swift (Payo's brother), and I entered a nameless village. I was seven years old, and we were in Suriname to attend a wedding. Naked children and dogs followed the dusty trail from our car. We pulled over to a big, flat, wooden house. In front was a large, heavy woman—even her ankles were fat, like a big leg of goat at the market.

Mayo shouted, "Gladys!" and they hugged and kissed. Auntie Gladys did the same to me. Auntie Gladys proceeded to squeeze my arms from my wrist to my collarbone. She squeezed me like the witch in "Hansel and Gretel" and looked at Payo and said they were not feeding me well and that I looked just like my mother, Reenie.

Payo and Uncle Swift left to join the village men, who were inside a grass hut with several hammocks. I saw a clear bottle of rum with no labels; they were drinking bush rum made by the local villagers. Uncle Swift knew how to make bush rum. I saw him doing it once with molasses, yeast, and buckets and buckets of rainwater that my brothers and I had to fetch for him.

As Mayo and I entered the dark kitchen, the flames from two dangling oil lamps were still, as if in a picture. A brown, naked baby boy was sleeping in a hammock in the kitchen. He was so tiny that he looked like a baby monkey my dad once brought home from the rain forest.

Several young women in the kitchen were busy chopping, cutting, grating coconuts, and peeling and deveining large, gray-colored shrimp. There were several hands of plantains hanging on iron hooks, bags of cassava, sweet potatoes in burlap bags, and heaps and heaps of green okra. On the black-smoked walls over the fireside stove, large pieces of catfish with heads on hung on a wire; they looked like starched clothing on a line. The fish were soaking up the gentle heat and light smoke from the wood fires below. On the burners of the fireside lay several silver pots. The flames left long soot marks. The pots bubbled away merrily, and occasionally the murky liquid escaped and made the amber coals hiss.

A young woman lifted the lid from one of the pots; a yellow and red habanero chile bobbed around like a dried coconut in the rough ocean. She grabbed a handful of whole baby okra and then two handfuls of deveined shrimp. She stirred the pot and covered it with the lid slightly ajar.

Mayo told Auntie Gladys that I cooked okra all the time, but I had never cooked okra whole, the way they were doing it. Mayo told Gladys how I always thinly sliced my okra and let it sun-dry for an hour on our zinc shed so it would not be slimly. I would then saute the okra in coconut oil, adding habanero chiles, shallots, and shrimp.

At dinnertime, we all sat around a large, wooden table underneath a blanket of stars. I sat on Uncle Swift's lap and watched as he struggled to eat the slimy *coo-coo* soup. It was delicious, but Uncle Swift was critical of the meal. I knew he did not like Mayo's side of the family, especially gossipy Auntie Gladys; Uncle Swift whispered in my ear that she was coo-coo, like the meal she made for us. He always knew how to make me laugh.

AFRICAN-STYLE BAKED COO-COO

{ serves 4 to 6 }

stuffed okra with shrimp

There are several versions of *coo-coo*: some are made into a stew or soup with varying ingredients, while others use a lot of cornmeal. But okra is always the star of this dish. This version is not mucouslike from the boiling of okras, nor is it deep-fried, which overcooks the okra. My brothers and I used to pick the okras from our trees in Guyana and eat them with salt and pepper. It's a delicate vegetable and needs to be treated that way. You will not be disappointed with this dish.

Olive oil cooking spray

Twenty 3–4-inch-long fresh okra, bottoms trimmed

5 oz cooked, peeled, and deveined shrimp, finely chopped

1 Tbsp yellow cornmeal

1 tsp curry powder

1 Tbsp finely chopped fresh cilantro

1 Tbsp canned unsweetened coconut milk or heavy cream

Sea salt

Freshly ground black pepper

1. Preheat the oven to 450°F. Grease a medium baking sheet with the cooking oil spray.

2. Using a knife, cut a slit along the length of each okra, being careful not to cut all the way through.

3. In a small mixing bowl, stir together the shrimp, cornmeal, curry powder, cilantro, coconut milk, and a pinch each of salt and pepper.

4. Carefully stuff each okra with about 1 tsp of filling and place on a baking sheet. Transfer to the top rack of the oven and bake for 5 minutes. Increase the oven temperature to broil (or transfer to broiler) and cook until the okra is lightly golden, about 3 minutes more. Serve Immediately.

Uncle Swift, Mayo, and Payo seemed to know everyone at the market in the port town of Nieuw Nickerie. Everywhere we stopped, people greeted us. Some gave Uncle Swift coils of money for his services, others offered hugs and handshakes. I was pinched on the cheek; rubbed on the head; lifted up and tossed in the air; kissed on my nose, cheeks, and forehead; and given gulden, the currency of Suriname.

We walked deeper into the market, passing whole sides of beef, goats, sheep, and pigs hanging on metal hooks. Chickens and ducks were packed in wire cages, price tags tied to their feet. Flies were buzzing everywhere. Next to the meat market was the fish market with heaps and heaps of gray-and yellow-bellied shrimp and tiny silver sardines. I thought to myself that the sardines needed a good dusting of curry powder and flour and should be deep-fried and eaten with a bowl of rice. There were shark, snook, mullet, high-water, catfish, *gilbaka*, and flying fish. The freshwater fish included *hassar*, *hoorie*, and tilapia.

A few minutes later we arrived at a massive food section. There were Chinese-looking people everywhere. Some were fair and some brown like me. They wore funny clothes; the men and women wore wraps around their waists. The women were beautiful, with long hair like my mother and me but tied up or braided.

The riot of smells from the food was like nothing I had ever encountered. The oil they cooked with was not coconut oil, and it smelled like roasted nuts. Uncle Swift said it was sesame seed oil from India. We arrived at a food stand with a gaudy, flowered plastic tablecloth. Flies hovered near some empty soda bottles. A jar of hot-pepper sauce sent the saliva in my mouth wild, like running raindrops on a lotus leaf.

A striking woman at the food stall saw Uncle Swift, removed her apron, and walked to meet us. After the greeting, we all sat down and a few other women brought us several types of dishes, including noodles piled high. There were several large bowls of piping-hot soup. Uncle Swift whirled the noodles with his fork, making sure to entwine the green long beans, and then stabbed the big, plump pink shrimp, dunking the fork into a heap of hot sauce on his plate. He looked at me, winked, and devoured the dish with relish.

I had never seen noodles served with shrimp before, only with chicken; it's how the Chinese in Guyana serve their lo-mein noodles. Uncle Swift twirled the yellow noodles again, and this time he fed me. He said that they were Java noodles, and that we were eating food from Java Island, Indonesia. He said that all the dark-skinned, Chinese-looking people with funny clothing I saw were from Java. The striking woman placed a bowl of soup in front of me. I could see the tiny beads of oil floating from the long hours of boiling in coconut milk. The soup was yellow from turmeric, and it had soft chunks of taro, plum-colored chicken feet, and a deep yellow yolk from a hard-boiled egg. The noodles were at the bottom of the bowl. It was my first time eating soup with noodles.

INDONESIAN BAMI GORENG

stir-fry noodles with chicken

If you can cook spaghetti with meatballs, you, too, can master this dish, impressing your friends and family with a delicious Indonesian delight.

Sea salt

½ lb fresh Asian-style egg noodles or spaghetti

3 Tbsp peanut oil

¾ lb chicken, cut into ¼-inch strips

1 Tbsp minced garlic

1 tsp peeled and minced fresh ginger

1 Tbsp tomato paste

2 Tbsp oyster sauce

½ cup hearts of palm, cut into matchstick strips

½ cup ½-inch pieces long beans or string beans

¼ cup light soy sauce

Freshly ground black pepper

½ cup 1-inch pieces green onion (*green part only*)

Fresh hot red chiles, thinly sliced, for garnish

1. Bring a large pot of water to a boil. Add 1 tsp salt and the egg noodles and cook until al dente, 3 to 5 minutes. Drain and rinse well under cold water. Set aside.

2. In a large skillet over medium heat, heat the peanut oil. When it is warm, not hot, add the chicken and cook, stirring constantly, for about 3 minutes. Add the garlic, ginger, tomato paste, and oyster sauce and cook, stirring, for 2 minutes more.

3. Add the hearts of palm and long beans. Continue to cook for 2 to 3 minutes more.

4. Increase the heat to high and add the soy sauce and cooked noodles. Stir and toss until the noodles are heated through. Season with salt and pepper. Add green onion, toss, and remove from the heat.

5. Serve immediately, garnished with the red chiles.

COCONUT-RASPBERRY BREAD & BUTTER PUDDING

{ serves 15 }

We were not fortunate enough to have wheat flour all the time in my house growing up, but when we did, we made *poori* and used the leftovers to make a pudding dish with milk. This is a more decadent version inspired by my childhood experience in Suriname.

18 slices *(about 1 loaf)* **challah or brioche bread**

1 cup fresh or frozen raspberries, thawed if frozen

4 cups canned evaporated milk

3 large eggs

1 cup granulated sugar

2 Tbsp vanilla extract

½ cup Cointreau or orange juice

1 Tbsp ground cinnamon

1 Tbsp freshly grated nutmeg

1 cup unsweetened shredded or grated coconut

½ cup packed demerara sugar or brown sugar

4 Tbsp unsalted butter, cubed

1. Arrange the bread slices in a lightly buttered 9-by-13-inch deep baking dish. Sprinkle ½ cup of the raspberries on top.

2. In a medium bowl, whisk the milk, eggs, granulated sugar, vanilla, Cointreau, cinnamon, nutmeg, and coconut. Pour over the bread.

3. Sprinkle the remaining raspberries on top, and press gently to help the bread absorb the liquid. Cover with two layers of aluminum foil and seal foil tightly around the edges of the baking dish. Let sit for 30 minutes.

4. While the bread sits, preheat the oven to 325°F.

5. Bake for 40 minutes. Remove the foil, sprinkle the pudding with the demerara sugar, and dot with the butter. Increase the oven temperature to 350°F.

6. Bake until the pudding is set and the top is golden brown, about 25 minutes more. Let cool slightly on a wire rack. Serve warm.

TO VENEZUELA

FRENCH GUIANA

CAYENNE

FROM SURINAME

It's hard to believe that perched at the northeastern shoulder of South America lies a French territory. Visiting French Guiana, with the euro as its currency, can be a surreal experience for some at first, because when we think of South America, Latin cultures come to mind.

Long, crusty baguettes peek out at you from shopping bags, and bakers' racks contain rows of buttery croissants. Market shelves hold my favorite Boursin cheese, and Peugeots and Renaults traverse the pothole-laden main roads and rough dirt roads of the countryside—all of which make you feel as if you are in a quaint neighborhood in Paris except for the occasional palm tree.

The original settlers of French Guiana, the Arawak and Carib tribes, still live in the territory's interior jungles. During the seventeenth century, the territory held brief settlements by the Dutch, French, and English, until in 1817 when France took full control of the territory. Today, immigrants from India, Malaysia, Vietnam, Indonesia, Haiti, and China add to this diverse French territory. In the 1970s, Hmong refugees from Laos settled in the countryside. In the small town of Cacao, you can find a small community of Laotian refugees; on weekends, they have a market with a bevy of exotic fruits and authentic Laotian food.

French Guiana's capital is Cayenne, home of the fiery red chile that bears its name. It's a colonial town with palm trees, wrought-iron rails, and colorful bustling markets that give it a cool, Caribbean feel. As for the local cuisine, well, each of the groups I mentioned adds to what is never a dull moment for your palate. I suggest trying out some of the food from street vendors. For me, street food is like Nirvana.

If you are an intrepid traveler, then French Guiana offers the adventure of a lifetime. I highly recommend taking a guided tour to explore the jungle, rivers, and rain forest. The thrill of this South American journey is staying in the tribal villages of the native Amerindians and Maroons, and sleeping in hammocks.

Besides its pristine rain forest, French Guiana is home to a space center run by Centre Spatial Guyanais (CSG) in partnership with the European Space Agency (ESA) and Arianespace. The space center quickly turned Kourou into a town full of space technicians, planet seekers, and stargazers. As a result, the local economy is booming. In fact, the revenue the space center generates for French Guiana makes for the highest per-capita income in South America.

Another attraction in Kourou is Île du Diable, Devil's Island, which housed a notorious penal colony until the mid-twentieth century. One of the most famous prisoners was murderer-turned-best-selling-author Henry Charrière, aka Papillon, whose story was made into a movie starring Steve McQueen and Dustin Hoffman.

FRENCH GUIANESE MENU

drink
TI RHUM PUNCH

soup
TARO, COCONUT MILK & CARDAMOM VICHYSSOISE

appetizer
YUCCA-TURMERIC SOUFFLÉ

main course
SARDINES STUFFED IN FRENCH BAGUETTES

dessert
CROQUEMBOUCHE WITH RUM & COCONUT

Anne, Auntie Lenine's daughter, took me by the hand and said that it was henna-painting time. Anne was the bride, and we were all preparing for the wedding.

Her room was packed with young girls, some of them mixing and then transferring the dark brown henna paste into plastic bags. The room smelled of guava and sandalwood. At the far corner of the room, some of the girls sat braced against colorful pillows. They were giggling and then smelling and sipping the guava drink as they passed the cup around. Anne took the cup and drank a big gulp. Then she held the cup to my mouth and the smell of rum ran up my nose, burning like a whiff of rubbing alcohol.

The guava nectar and cloves had been simmering for hours and were now mixed into a rum punch. No wonder the girls were giggling. I took a sip; it was bitter from the rum. I thought that if a little less rum had been put in the drink, it would have tasted better because guava with cloves is so good.

After several sips of rum and guava punch, my head was twirling. The girls were painting me with henna, fixing my hair, and putting all sorts of jewelry on me like I was their little doll. That evening, I fell asleep to the jingles of bangles and the giggles of girls.

TI RHUM PUNCH

{ serves 2 }

Guava nectar works quite nicely in this drink, but I sometimes use peach juice for an equally delicious alternative.

2 cups guava nectar or juice

⅛ tsp ground ginger

⅛ tsp ground cloves or nutmeg

4 oz dark rum

Ice

Fresh mint for garnish

1. In a cocktail shaker, combine the guava nectar, ginger, cloves, and rum. Stir until the spices are dissolved. Add 1 cup of ice and shake vigorously.

2. Divide between 2 tumblers filled with more ice. Garnish with the mint. Serve immediately.

TARO, COCONUT MILK & CARDAMOM VICHYSSOISE

{ serves 4 to 6 }

This chilled soup simply corrupted my palate—in a good way; it made me think outside of the box about the possibilities of how food can be prepared. Throughout my travels around the globe, I have had many versions of vichyssoise, but I continue to make this version, which stained my taste buds at the age of seven.

2 Tbsp unsalted butter

1 cup thinly sliced leeks (*white portion only*)

2 large shallots, thinly sliced

Sea salt

1 lb taro, peeled and thinly sliced

4 cups low-sodium chicken stock, plus more if needed

½ cup canned unsweetened coconut milk

⅛ tsp ground cardamom, plus more for garnish

Ground white pepper

Fresh chives for garnish

1. In a large saucepan over medium heat, melt the butter. Sauté the leeks, shallots, and a pinch of salt. Cook until tender but not brown. Add the taro and chicken stock and bring to a boil. Cover, reduce the heat, and simmer for 35 minutes.

2. Working in batches, purée the mixture in a food processor. Return the purée to the saucepan. If needed, add more stock to reach the desired consistency.

3. Add the coconut milk and ⅛ tsp cardamom, mixing well. Season with salt and white pepper. Serve hot, or cover and refrigerate and serve well chilled. Ladle into bowls, garnish with the chives and a tiny pinch of ground cardamom, and serve.

When I awoke on the day of the wedding with a pain in my head and a burning in my throat, Auntie Lenine fed me a thick, cold liquid. I wanted to spit it out, but I thought that would be disrespectful. She said her mother used to make this soup all the time in France. She kept shoving spoonfuls of chilled soup in my mouth as she spoke endlessly about her mother and her daughter, Anne.

All I could think of was what Uncle Swift had said about white French people. He said that they cook things and put them in the refrigerator because they don't like to cook every day. Payo, my grandfather, would have said that hot soup was the best.

But, several more spoonfuls later, my taste buds adapted to the cold soup. It would have been better if I had brushed my teeth, though. It was the fanciest soup I had ever had. I tasted shallots and taro, and the coconut milk made it rich and creamy.

In the market, a large, heavy woman called to Mayo, my grandmother. We turned around to find a lady seated under a large blue umbrella, bouncing a baby boy in her lap. Mayo smiled, called out to her cousin Mona, and happily walked over to her. Mayo left me behind, but I followed dodging cars.

Tiny beads of sweat lay on Mona's forehead, which was framed by her salt-and-pepper hair. She looked about my mother's age, but the sun had damaged her. Her skin had no moisture, as she had given it all to her baby, who was glistening black from coconut oil.

Mona was selling lots of food, which I could smell. The food was covered under a clean, white cloth on her table. I sat down on the bench under the large umbrella and tried to look under the cloth. But I knew Mayo was looking at me out of the corner of her eye.

Mona eventually removed the white cloth and exposed a sea of gold and orange in rows, looking like the marigolds in our yard. The aroma of sweet onions simmered for hours overtook my senses. The rows of calabash squash bowls were filled with orange-colored soup, with pieces of chicken meat bobbing on top. Gold-colored, breadlike custards with specks of brown and smooth tops looked pretty in small, chipped white enamel bowls.

Mona handed me a calabash squash bowl with a spoon. Mashed sweet pumpkin with a touch of curry powder, cumin, and onions spread in my mouth like wildfire, and then the aftertaste of cayenne pepper set my mouth ablaze. There were also sardines with minced red onions stuffed into a long, skinny bread.

I sampled one of the custards. The marriage of garlic and mashed yucca had never tasted so delicious. I did not know that yucca could be so smooth. I would always boil and fry it for a few minutes. Mona's custard was smooth, like cake batter, and the eggs in it made it fluffy. It was warm, with no spices, and it calmed my burning mouth.

Mona said that she learned how to make the soufflé from a French woman for whom she had worked. The French woman made it with potatoes and sometimes cheese. Mona said it's usually fluffier when it comes out of the oven and that you should eat it right away.

YUCCA-TURMERIC SOUFFLÉ {serves 6 to 8}

Since childhood, this dish has been a favorite in our home. My grandmother made it almost every weekend after our visit to French Guiana.

7 Tbsp unsalted butter

1 lb yucca, peeled and cut into 1-inch pieces *(see note)*

Sea salt

Ground white pepper

1 cup whole milk

½ tsp ground turmeric

3 small egg yolks, beaten

5 small egg whites

Finely chopped chives for garnish

NOTE Yucca is sold frozen or fresh. If using fresh, remove the tough skin, split the yucca in half, and remove the fibrous vein. If using frozen, remove the fibrous vein.

1 Preheat the oven to 375°F. Grease a 2-quart soufflé dish with 1 Tbsp butter.

2 Place the yucca in a medium saucepan, add a pinch of salt, and enough cold water to cover by 2 inches. Bring to a boil over medium heat and cook until fork-tender, 30 to 35 minutes. Drain. Transfer to a medium bowl. While still hot, force the yucca through a ricer or food mill. Discard any tough fibers. Season the mashed yucca with salt and white pepper.

3 In a large saucepan over very low heat, whisk together the milk and turmeric. Bring to a low simmer, add the remaining 6 Tbsp of butter, and continue to whisk until the butter has melted. Gradually whisk in the mashed yucca until it's smooth and there are no lumps. Gradually pour in the egg yolks and continue to whisk. Remove from the heat and allow to cool completely.

4 Meanwhile, in large bowl, beat the egg whites with a pinch of salt using an electric mixer at high speed until stiff peaks form. (After the beaters are lifted, stiff peaks should remain; when the bowl is tilted, the egg whites should not slide.)

5 Using a rubber spatula, stir one-third of the beaten egg whites into the cooled yucca mixture. Fold in another one-third of the egg whites by gently cutting down to the bottom of the saucepan, scraping up the side of the pan, then folding over the top of mixture. Repeat until all egg whites are incorporated into the yucca mixture.

6 Pour the yucca mixture into the prepared dish, gently smoothing the top. Bake until the soufflé puffs up to the rim of dish, the center is set, and the top is lightly browned, 45 to 50 minutes. Serve hot, sprinkled with chives.

SARDINES STUFFED IN FRENCH BAGUETTES

Not only is this a famous street food in French Guiana, but I have had it in both Suriname and Guyana. Some versions aren't cooked, but I like it cooked, and it hits the spot right around lunchtime. I prepare canned tuna this way, too.

3 Tbsp extra-virgin olive oil

2 large shallots, thinly sliced

1 Tbsp chopped garlic

2 small fresh red jalapeño or cayenne chiles, seeded and finely chopped

One 16-oz can sardines packed in tomato sauce

2 Tbsp finely chopped fresh oregano

2 Tbsp finely chopped fresh parsley

1 Tbsp freshly squeezed lime juice

Sea salt

One 12-inch-long baguette, halved crosswise and sliced open horizontally

Lettuce leaves (optional)

Slices of tomato (optional)

1. In a small saucepan, heat the olive oil over medium-high heat. Add the shallots, garlic, and chiles and cook until soft, about 3 minutes. Add the sardines with their sauce, oregano, parsley, and lime juice. Stir well, mashing up sardines, and cook for 5 minutes more. Season with salt. Remove from the heat and set aside.

2. Make sandwiches by spreading the sardine mixture on the bottoms of the bread, adding the lettuce and tomatoes (if using), and replacing the tops. Slice into smaller sandwiches, if you like. Serve immediately.

French Guiana's countryside was much like our villages in Guyana. Wooden plank houses with zinc roofs dotted one section of a village, which gave way to green rice fields and banana plantations. The sand on the dams was the color of the morning sunset. We passed rich people's homes, which were made of concrete and painted bright white. Their yards were well maintained often with several fruit trees.

Auntie Lenine is French; her hair is reddish brown like the color of a coconut shell. My brothers and I called her "the white lady" because her skin is fair and custard-like, similar to the flesh of the lady guavas we had in our yard in Guyana.

I was very excited to help her make her daughter's wedding cake. When we walked into the kitchen, I noticed that many of the ingredients had already been prepared by several women. They stood aside as they watched what Auntie Lenine was doing. She asked me to help her throw the flour into the large mixing bowl. The other bowls contained grated coconut, milk, brown sugar, burnt sugar syrup, butter, eggs, and tonka beans (which look like raisins but taste like vanilla beans). I noticed the unusual spelling on the bottle of rum on the table: *rhum*.

As Auntie Lenine added water and butter to the flour mixture, she said that our cake was going to look like a mountain, not like regular round, flat cakes. We were going to make small puffed balls, like Ping-Pong balls, which we were going to use to build the mountain. She said that was how her mother made her wedding cake in France.

It took us five hours to make Anne's wedding cake. We stuffed the puffed balls with a sweet coconut-and-rum mixture and then stacked them up to build a small mountain. We used burnt sugar to bind them together. Some of the women made flowers out of almond paste and used pomegranate syrup to color them blood-red. These were neatly tucked between the puffed pastries. Anne's cake looked magical—just like a mountain with wild red flowers. The thin ribbons of sugar cascaded like summer rain glistening in the sunlight.

CROQUEMBOUCHE
WITH RUM & COCONUT

{ serves 12 to 15 }

This French wedding cake consists of a conical heap of *choux* (buns), which are hollow and can
be filled with cream. The buns are bound together with a caramel sauce. It's usually dotted with
flowers; I've used lavender in other versions. The name *croquembouche* comes from the French
words meaning "crunch in the mouth." You will need a croquembouche mold for this recipe,
available at well-stocked cookware stores and specialty cake-supply stores.

PÂTE À CHOUX

1½ cups all-purpose flour

2 cups water

1 cup (2 sticks) butter

1 Tbsp salt

9 medium eggs, or as needed

2 large egg yolks

COCONUT-RUM PASTRY CREAM

3 cups canned unsweetened coconut milk

¾ cup sugar

¾ cup (1½ sticks) unsalted butter

1 vanilla bean, halved lengthwise, seeds scraped out and bean reserved

6 large egg yolks

½ cup cornstarch

1 Tbsp rum

2 Tbsp finely grated coconut

CARAMEL SAUCE

1½ cups water

3 cups sugar

2 Tbsp corn syrup

Crystallized and/or fresh flowers for decorating

1 Preheat the oven to 400°F. Lightly grease four large baking sheets and set aside.

2 To make the *pâte à choux*: sift flour into a large bowl. Set aside.

3 In a large saucepan over medium heat, combine the water, butter, and salt and bring to a simmer. Remove from the heat, add the flour, and stir with a wooden spoon until the mixture is smooth and pulls away from sides of the pan and the dough forms a ball. Return the pan to the stove and cook over low heat, stirring until warmed through, 1 to 2 minutes.

4 Remove from the heat, let cool slightly, and then transfer the dough to the bowl of an electric mixer fitted with a paddle attachment. Beat in 6 of the eggs. Add the remaining 3 eggs, one at a time, mixing well after each addition. You do not want the batter to become runny; if it does, stop adding eggs. The dough should hold a string if you pinch some between your fingers and spread them apart.

5 In a small bowl or shallow cup, mix the egg yolks with 2 Tbsp water for an egg wash. Set aside.

6 Spoon the batter into a large piping bag fitted with a ½-inch plain round pastry tip. Cover any remaining batter with a damp cloth or plastic wrap to prevent a skin from forming. Pipe ¾- to 1-inch mounds onto the prepared baking sheets, spaced about 2 inches apart. Press the peaks down onto the mounds using a moistened fingertip and brush with the egg wash.

7 Bake in batches until firm and hollow-sounding when tapped, about 20 minutes. You can reduce the oven temperature to 300°F when the puffs' color is golden brown.

8 Transfer the *choux* to wire racks and let cool completely. Using the tip of a sharp knife, make a small hole in the bottom of each puff. Set aside.

continued

9. To make the pastry cream: In a medium saucepan, combine the coconut milk, sugar, butter, and vanilla seeds and bean. Bring to a simmer over medium heat.

10. In a medium bowl, combine the egg yolks and cornstarch and whisk to dissolve the cornstarch.

11. Gradually, while whisking to combine, pour the warm coconut milk mixture over the egg yolk mixture.

12. Return the mixture to a clean saucepan and cook over medium heat, stirring constantly until thick, 2 to 5 minutes. Remove from the heat, discard the vanilla bean, and pass the mixture through a fine-mesh sieve into a bowl. Cover closely with plastic wrap and refrigerate until the mixture is chilled and firm, about 2 hours.

13. Using an electric mixer, beat the chilled pastry cream until smooth. Add the rum and grated coconut. Spoon the pastry cream into a piping bag fitted with a 1-inch pastry tip.

14. Insert the tip into hole of each *choux* puff and pipe in enough cream to fill. Set aside.

15. To make the caramel sauce: In a large heavy-bottomed saucepan, combine the water, sugar, and corn syrup. Bring to a boil over high heat without stirring. Cook until the mixture reaches 312°F or hard-crack stage on a candy thermometer, 20 to 25 minutes. Remove immediately from the heat so the mixture doesn't continue cooking. (You want to make the caramel *only* when you are ready to assemble the final *croquembouche*. If the caramel gets too thick, return the pan to a low heat to thin it.)

16 Place the *croquembouche* mold (see recipe introduction), point down, on a work surface and lightly grease the inside.

17 Using tongs, dip the bottom half of a *choux* in the caramel and place, caramel side up, into the point of the cone. Using the caramel as an adhesive, arrange a ring of *choux* on top of the puff at the point of the cone. Continue building rings of *choux* up the walls of the mold until the mold is covered. Use only enough caramel to adhere the *choux* to each other. If the caramel begins to harden, return the pan to a low heat to thin it.

18 Allow the *croquembouche* to cool about 5 minutes to set the caramel. Place a serving platter over the base of the mold, then carefully flip the mold so that the pyramid is upright. Carefully remove the mold from the *croquembouche*.

19 Decorate with crystallized and fresh flowers. You can also dip a fork into the remaining caramel and drizzle over the *croquembouche* for a spun-sugar effect.

FROM
FRENCH GUIANA

CARACAS

VENEZUELA

TO FALKLAND ISLANDS

T he incredible spectacle of Angel Falls is nestled in the jungles of Venezuela, deep within the Guiana Highlands, a rocky upland region south of the Orinoco delta. Long before you get a glimpse, you can hear the thundering roar of the stupendous force of millions of tons of water. The freshwater falls plunge off the edge of Auyán-tepuí or Devil's Mountain, a *tepuí* (tabletop mountain) with a stunning uninterrupted drop.

Apart from Angel Falls, this oil-rich country is a land of white sandy Caribbean beaches and snowcapped Andean peaks. Venezuela is bordered by Guyana to the east, Colombia to the west, and Brazil to the south. The region is fantastically rich not only in flora and fauna but also in minerals such as gold and bauxite.

The original Amerindians of Venezuela were very primitive, unlike others of the Andean region, and there were no great indigenous civilizations. Around 2000 B.C., some of the Amerindians settled along the *llanos* (plains) and eventually developed a more stable lifestyle as the population around them grew.

Christopher Columbus landed in Venezuela in 1498, when, by accident, he came to the mouth of the Orinoco River. The Spanish christened the land "Venezuela," meaning "Little Venice," after seeing the Amerindian homes sitting on wooden stilts above the water.

Unlike its varied natural landscapes, Venezuela's cuisine is simple. Most of it is borrowed from the nearby Caribbean. In the Venezuelan kitchen, you will find staples such as coconuts, mangoes, papayas, guavas, avocados, and bananas. There is also an abundance of seafood; and a Venezuela meal is not complete without *caviar criollo* (mashed black beans). Corn is used to make every Venezuelan's favorite street food, *arepas*. These corn cakes are a bit thicker than Mexican tortillas and are often cooked by heating them on a grill, like pancakes. They can be sweet, savory, plain, or stuffed.

Today in the metropolitan city of Caracas you will find a mixture of Amerindians, along with Africans and Europeans—particularly German immigrants, who settled there in the early 1900s. We can thank the culinary gods for that, because the Germans brought techniques for making great cheeses and *cervezas* (beer). To me, an *arepa* would not taste the same unless accompanied with cheese and a chilled *cerveza* proudly made in Venezuela.

VENEZUELAN MENU

drink
PAPELÓN CON LIMÓN
sugarcane & lime juice drink

soup
CREAM OF SWEET POTATO SOUP WITH PLANTAIN CHIPS

salad
PUMPKIN & STRING BEAN SALAD

appetizer
GUASACACA CON CHIFLES
green tomato & avocado dip with chips

main course
PASTICHO
lasagna with red sauce & white coconut milk sauce

dessert
CACHAPAS CON FRUTAS
corn cakes with blackberry compote

The capital of Venezuela, Caracas, is one of the most urbanized cities in South America. There are barrios of homes painted colors like the feathers of a peacock clinging haphazardly to the rocky hillside.

In the middle of one dirt-road-laden rancho, I sought refuge from the 110-degree temperature under a towering tamarind tree. I sat against its brown rugged bark, into which were etched the names of lovers and dates. As I fanned myself with my cap, I wondered what happened to those lovers.

My daydream was disturbed by laughter and shouting. Two boys about eight years old waved at me then returned to kicking a half-deflated soccer ball. The dust from their play suspended in the air and glistened like the dust of gold. There was no wind, and I continued to perspire. In the neighbor's yard, a few tall papaya and guava trees stood tall, basking in the sunshine. The bottled water in my backpack was warm. I needed something chilled. And, suddenly, as if a genie just popped up to grant my wish, I heard the ringing of a bicycle bell. For a street-food eater, that's the sound of life, hope, and merriment. Whenever I hear that *ding*, I know my appetite will be satisfied—and no doubt with something unexpected.

My discovery that day was an elixir called *papelón con limón*, the preferred street drink in Venezuela.

PAPELÓN CON LIMÓN

sugarcane & lime juice drink

This refreshing beverage is made with raw, hardened sugarcane pulp, water, and lime juice, which is then strained and served chilled. Street vendors serve it everywhere—it's practically the national drink—in the typical manner: in a plastic bag with a straw. Sugarcane juice can be found in Latin and West Indian markets.

1½ cups canned
sugarcane juice

2 Tbsp freshly squeezed
lime juice

2 tsp superfine sugar

Crushed ice

Lime twists for garnish

1. In a medium pitcher, combine the sugarcane juice, lime juice, and sugar. Stir until the sugar is dissolved. Divide the mixture between 2 highball glasses.

2. Add the ice, stir, and serve each glass garnished with a lime twist.

CREAM OF SWEET POTATO SOUP WITH PLANTAIN CHIPS

This soup is divine on a cold winter's night. It's a vegetarian's delight, and it also freezes well. The plantain chips are a great snack for kids—or adults: One of my favorite things to do is dip them into peanut butter. Leftovers can be stored in airtight plastic containers.

3 Tbsp extra-virgin olive oil

1 medium onion, finely chopped

1 tsp minced garlic

Sea salt

1 tsp sweet paprika

⅛ tsp ground annatto

1 tsp ground cumin

⅛ tsp ground turmeric

2 cups peeled and diced sweet potato (*1 large potato, about 14 oz*)

3 cups low-sodium vegetable stock

One 14-oz can unsweetened coconut milk

Freshly ground black pepper

Plaintain Chips (*facing page*) for serving

2 Tbsp chopped fresh parsley for garnish

1. In a large saucepan, heat olive oil over medium-low heat. Add the onion, garlic, and a pinch of salt. Sauté until soft, stirring frequently, about 2 minutes. Add the paprika, annatto, cumin, and turmeric and cook for 1 minute more, stirring frequently.

2. Add the sweet potato and stir constantly for 1 minute more. Add the stock and coconut milk and bring to a boil. Reduce the heat to low and cover. Simmer until the potato is fork-tender, 15 to 20 minutes. Season with salt and pepper. Using a hand blender, blend until smooth, or transfer to a food processor and blend.

3. Ladle the soup into 4 bowls and top each with a plantain chip. Sprinkle on the parsley and serve immediately. Pass out the remaining chips at the table.

PLANTAIN CHIPS

{ makes about 40 chips }

Vegetable oil for frying

4 large green plantains *(skin should be green and firm)*, **peeled** *(see note)*

Coarse sea salt

1. In a heavy skillet over medium-high heat, heat enough oil for deep-frying (about 4 inches) until a deep-fry thermometer reads 365°F.

2. Cut each plaintain in half crosswise, then cut lengthwise into thin slices no thicker than ⅛-inch. Carefully drop the plantain slices into the hot oil, about six at a time, and cook, turning occasionally until they are golden brown on both sides, 3 to 4 minutes. Drain on a plate lined with paper towels and immediately sprinkle with sea salt. Serve immediately.

NOTE To peel plantains, working with one fruit at a time, use a sharp knife to score the skin down the entire length. Lightly oil your hands so that the sap does not stain them. Use your fingers to peel off the skin, then use the knife to trim off any skin that clings to the flesh. Makes about 40 chips.

PUMPKIN & STRING BEAN SALAD

{serves 2}

This is a rather unusual salad, and I like it. I had something similar on Margarita Island. That salad came with molasses; I thought it really brought out the flavor of the pumpkin, which is not very sweet. The pumpkin seeds give this healthful, protein-rich salad a nice crunch.

2 cups peeled ½-inch diced pumpkin

Sea salt

½ lb fresh slender green beans, trimmed and cut into 1-inch pieces

3 Tbsp extra-virgin olive oil

1 tsp freshly squeezed lime juice

3 Tbsp blackstrap molasses or honey

⅛ tsp cayenne pepper

1 small shallot, sliced

½ cup shelled unsalted pumpkin seeds (pepitas)

Freshly ground black pepper

Shredded coconut, for garnish (optional)

Place the pumpkin in a large saucepan. Add a pinch of salt and add enough cold water to cover by 1 inch. Bring to a boil over medium heat and cook until just tender, about 2 minutes. Remove from the heat and add the green beans. Cover and let steep for 1 minute more.

Transfer to a colander and drain in a sink. Immediately run under cold water for 30 seconds. Let stand to drain.

Meanwhile, in a large bowl, whisk together the olive oil, lime juice, molasses, cayenne, and shallot. Add the drained pumpkin and beans and the pumpkin seeds to bowl and lightly toss. Season with salt and pepper.

Divide the salad between 2 salad bowls or plates and sprinkle with the coconut (if using). Serve immediately.

NOTE This salad can be made ahead and refrigerated.

GUASACACA CON CHIFLES

serves 6 to 8

green tomato & avocado dip with chips

Long before I tasted this dish in Venezuela, I was making it as a little girl in Guyana. We had an abundance of plantain and avocado trees in our yard, so I had lots of time to experiment with those two ingredients. When the plantains are double-fried, the resulting chips are known as *tostónes*, or *patacónes* in certain Latin American countries and Caribbean islands. But when fried just once, these treats are called *chifles* in Venezuela. The guasacaca dip is also delicious with yucca fries.

6 small ripe avocados, halved, pitted, and flesh scooped from skin and roughly chopped *(see note)*

Sea salt

1 tsp red pepper flakes

2 small shallots, thinly sliced

2 Tbsp freshly squeezed lime juice

1 cup ¼-inch-dice green tomatoes

¼ cup finely chopped fresh cilantro

Freshly ground black pepper

Plaintain Chips *(page 101)* or Yucca Fries *(page 177)* for serving

1. In a small bowl, combine the avocado flesh and 1 tps salt and mash coarsely with a fork. Add the red pepper flakes, shallots, and lime juice and mix well.

2. Gently fold in the green tomatoes and cilantro. Season with salt and pepper.

3. Serve immediately with the Plantain Chips or Yucca Fries.

NOTE To easily remove the pit of an avocado, cut lengthwise all the way around the whole avocado, then twist the halves to separate. Firmly hit the pit with a knife so that it embeds into it, then gently twist the knife until the pit pops out. Scoop out the flesh with a spoon.

PASTICHO

lasagna with red sauce & white coconut milk sauce

This dish is a form of lasagna traditionally found in Venezuela and Colombia. It's different from the Italian version, and it will blow your mind. Don't use sauce from a jar or bottle, please; make this from scratch, and you will not be disappointed.

RED SAUCE

⅓ cup extra-virgin olive oil

1 large onion, finely chopped

2 Tbsp minced garlic

2 Tbsp finely chopped
fresh oregano

Sea salt

1 lb lean ground beef

1 lb chorizo, cut into
¼-inch dice

1 Tbsp red pepper flakes

2 tsp chopped fresh thyme

2 tsp ground cumin

Two 28-oz cans crushed
tomatoes with added purée

Freshly ground black pepper

1. To make the red sauce: In a large, heavy pot, heat the olive oil over medium-high heat. Add the onion, garlic, oregano, and a pinch of salt. Sauté until soft, stirring frequently, about 2 minutes.

2. Add the beef, chorizo, red pepper flakes, thyme, and cumin and cook for 10 minutes more, stirring frequently. Add the crushed tomatoes. Reduce the heat to medium and simmer for 8 minutes more.

3. Season with salt and pepper. Remove the sauce from the heat and set aside to cool.

COCONUT MILK SAUCE

½ cup *(1 stick)* unsalted butter

¼ cup minced shallots

1 Tbsp minced garlic

¼ cup all-purpose flour

3 cups canned unsweetened coconut milk

Salt

Freshly ground black pepper

½ cup julienned fresh basil leaves

16 oz no-boil lasagna noodles

4 cups freshly grated mozzarella cheese

1½ cups freshly grated Parmesan cheese

To make the coconut milk sauce: In a large saucepan over low heat, melt the butter. Add the shallots and garlic and sauté until soft, about 5 minutes. Gradually sprinkle in the flour and whisk until smooth.

Gradually whisk in the coconut milk and then whisk constantly until the sauce thickens. Keep whisking 2 minutes more. Season with salt and pepper. Add the basil.

Remove the sauce from heat and set aside to cool.

Preheat the oven to 350°F. Spread one-fifth of the red sauce on the bottom of a 15-by-10-by-2-inch glass baking dish. Arrange the first layer of approximately 3 to 4 noodles atop sauce.

Add one-fourth of the coconut milk sauce and spread out evenly to cover the noodles. Use your hands if necessary to spread out, as the white sauce can be a bit thick. Add another portion of red sauce. Sprinkle on about 1 cup of the mozzarella cheese and about ¼ cup of the Parmesan cheese.

Repeat the layers of noodles, red sauce, coconut milk sauce, and cheeses. Top with the remaining noodles. Spoon any remaining sauces atop noodles. Sprinkle with any remaining cheeses. Bake the lasagna for 1 hour until lightly golden and juices are bubbling around edges. Remove from the oven and let stand for 10 minutes before serving.

I was on my way to the hot springs of Termales las Trincheras. Passing through the highland city of Valencia, I met a lovely, moon-shaped woman, Yasabel, at a local market. She was selling some of the most beautiful hand-embroidered handkerchiefs I have ever seen. They reminded me of how my mother tried to domesticate me by teaching me how to sew on our Singer. I am afraid it's a talent I never mastered—cooking was enough for me.

Yasabel showed me how to embroider and, of course, I giggled more than my fingers could work. She asked what I did for a living, which led to an invitation to her home for dinner. The meal Yasabel prepared for me was an adventure. In her *pasticho*, she used slices of ham and ground rabbit and pork. She also made her red and white sauces separately and from scratch.

CACHAPAS CON FRUTAS

{ makes 12 *cachapas*; serves 4 }

corn cakes with blackberry compote

Venezuela's *cachapas* are a comfort food enjoyed by all the locals. These corn cakes can be made into savory snacks by adding mozzarella cheese, or, when stuffed like a sandwich with eggs and bacon, they make a wonderful breakfast treat. I've also had sweet versions, such as with *mora* jam, South America's blackberry.

1½ cups whole milk

6 Tbsp unsalted butter, plus more for pan

½ cup buttermilk

2 cups frozen corn kernels, thawed

2 cups finely ground yellow cornmeal

½ cup sugar

½ tsp salt

2 cups grated Havarti or Monterey Jack cheese

BLACKBERRY COMPOTE

2 cups fresh blackberries, rinsed

½ cup sugar

1 Tbsp grated orange zest

1 tsp ground ginger

1 tsp cornstarch, dissolved in 1½ Tbsp chilled orange juice or cold water

Honey or maple syrup, for drizzling

Fresh mint for garnish

1. In a medium saucepan, bring the milk to a boil over high heat. Remove from the heat and let sit for 3 minutes. Add the 6 Tbsp butter and the buttermilk. Stir until the butter has completely melted, then let sit for 3 minutes.

2. Pulse the corn kernels in a food processor until just coarse. In a large mixing bowl, combine the corn, cornmeal, sugar, salt, and cheese and mix well. Gradually add enough of the warm milk mixture to make a very thick batter.

3. Heat a griddle or large skillet over medium-high heat and melt about 1 Tbsp of the butter. When the foam subsides, drop about 2 Tbsp of the batter onto the skillet for each *cachapa* (they should be about 3 inches in diameter). Cook until the underside is golden brown, about 4 minutes, then turn and cook until brown on the second side. Continue to cook the remaining cachapas and cover with a clean towel until ready to serve.

4. To make the blackberry compote: In a medium saucepan over medium heat, combine the blackberries, sugar, orange zest, and ginger. Bring to a slow simmer, add the dissolved cornstarch, and cook until the mixture begins to thicken. Remove from heat and let cool to warm before serving.

5. Stack 13 of the *cachapas*, drizzle with honey or syrup, and add the compote. Garnish with a sprig of mint and serve warm.

STANLEY

FALKLAND
ISLANDS

I f there is a place on Earth that truly makes you feel as if you have landed on another planet, it is the Falkland Islands. It almost seems as if the Falklands—with borders of white, sandy beaches; crisp, clear azure skies; a vast, open ocean with an endless horizon; and a night sky that looks like scattered diamonds—are tucked away at the edge of the universe.

Since the early 1800s, Argentina has laid claim to the islands, which had been occupied and administered by the British. In 1982, Argentina invaded the islands but was quickly defeated by the British; today the area is considered a self-governing overseas territory of the United Kingdom.

Also known to Argentines as Isla Malvinas the Falklands are a group of two hundred islands. The two main islands, East and West Falkland, are about three hundred miles off the east coast of Argentina. East Falkland is only about 2,550 square miles. Once you leave its capital, Stanley, the landscape of the island changes dramatically to pristine rock-strewn beauty, grassy knolls, abundant flora and fauna, and numerous hamlets, coves, and beaches teeming with wildlife. Many small settlements are scattered about the countryside, although there are some touristy remnants of the island's battles, like the Argentine cemetery in Goose Green or the British cemetery in San Carlos. Everything on the island is British, including Land Rovers, red telephone booths, driving on the left, tea time, and warm peat fires burning in every hearth.

As for food in the Falklands, just think of the whole island as an organic compound. The natives take their foods seriously, and everything is fresh. Local organic sheep farms powered by wind turbines dot the lush, green valleys. These sheep are used in the most tender lamb dishes, which just melt in your mouth. Seafood is also abundant, and most of it is exported to other countries. A favorite local fish is mullet, which is basically Atlantic cod. It is a meaty fish that one can never have enough of. However, don't get your culinary hopes too high: There is no new "ethnic" cooking style. Rather, it is pure Brit comfort food, since most of the residents are of British descent.

FALKLAND ISLANDS MENU

appetizer
BAKED CURRY
FISH & CHIPS

main course
LAMB & RUTABAGA
COTTAGE PIE

BAKED CURRY FISH & CHIPS {serves 6 to 8}

I don't like my fish deep-fried, so I've altered the recipe I savored in the Falklands by baking it. I also bake my chicken fingers; you can substitute chicken for the fish here and follow the same recipe—just bake for 5 minutes longer. If you can't live without curry (like me), you will love every bite of this dish.

2 Tbsp curry powder

1 tsp freshly squeezed lemon juice

1 tsp peeled and minced fresh ginger

1 tsp minced garlic

¼ tsp salt

2 lb firm fish fillets, such as cod or halibut, cut into 1-inch-wide strips

Nonstick cooking spray

¼ cup all-purpose flour

2 large eggs, beaten

2 cups panko bread crumbs

Lime wedges for garnish

Your favorite dipping sauce, such as tartar sauce, ketchup, or sweet and sour sauce for serving

Plaintain Chips *(page 101)* or Yucca Fries *(page 177)* for serving

1. In a large bowl, mix together the curry powder, lemon juice, ginger, garlic, and salt. Add the fish and turn to coat on all sides. (This can be done a few hours in advance, if desired.)

2. Preheat the oven to 375°F and line a baking sheet with parchment paper or foil. Spray with the nonstick cooking spray and set aside.

3. Dredge the fish in the flour and shake off excess. Dip into the beaten eggs, then press into the bread crumbs, making sure to coat on all sides.

4. Place the fish on the prepared baking sheet and bake until golden, about 10 minutes.

5. Garnish with the lime wedges and serve immediately with dipping sauce and chips.

LAMB & RUTABAGA COTTAGE PIE

{ serves 6–8 }

Rutabagas are cheaper than potatoes and have a texture that is unbelievably delicious in this hearty meal.

2½ lb rutabaga, peeled and cut into 1-inch pieces

4 Tbsp unsalted butter, melted

Sea salt

Freshly ground black pepper

2 Tbsp extra-virgin olive oil

2 lb ground lamb

1 Tbsp minced garlic

1 large onion, finely chopped

1 Tbsp curry powder

1 tsp cayenne pepper

2 Tbsp tomato paste

¼ cup vegetable stock

1 cup shelled fresh peas

2 celery stalks, cut into ½-inch-thick slices

½ cup finely chopped carrot

2 Tbsp freshly grated Parmesan cheese

1. In a large saucepan, combine the rutabaga and enough cold salted water to cover by 1 inch. Bring to a boil, uncovered, and cook until fork-tender, about 30 to 35 minutes. Drain in a colander and lay on a baking sheet lined with paper towels. Let sit for 5 minutes. Force the rutabaga through a ricer. Discard any tough fibers.

2. In the same saucepan over high heat, whisk the mashed rutabaga constantly for 5 minutes so any water is absorbed and the rutabaga is the texture of mashed potatoes. Add the melted butter and whisk for 1 minute more. Season with salt and pepper. Remove from the heat and set aside.

3. Preheat the oven to 350°F.

4. In a 2½-quart heavy cast-iron skillet over medium heat, heat the olive oil. Add the ground lamb and cook, stirring frequently, until a bit brown, 5 to 8 minutes. Add the garlic, onion, and a pinch of salt. Cook, stirring, for about 2 minutes more. Add the curry powder, cayenne, and tomato paste and cook for 1 minute more. Add the stock, peas, celery, and carrot. Bring to a boil, stirring frequently, and cook until all the liquid is absorbed, scraping up any brown bits. Season with salt and pepper.

5. Remove the skillet from the heat. Increase the oven temperature to broil.

6. Spoon the rutabaga mixture over the cooked lamb and spread evenly using a whisk, making a rough surface. Sprinkle with the cheese. Broil about 3 inches from the heat source until the top is golden, about 3 minutes. Serve warm.

nirmala's edible diary

I entered the dark, smoke-filled pub—it was the only pollution I noticed in the Falkland Islands. In the back of Glove Tavern in the town of Stanley was a jukebox blasting David Bowie. I sat at a table and a young waitress came over. Her face showed the telltale signs of the number of cigarettes she had smoked. She was dressed in black skin-tight suede, which crushed her rather large, voluptuous breasts. On her right hip rested the dusty chalkboard menu, which read Fish and Chips, Cottage Pies, Kidney Pies, and Pâté. "No curry," I sighed to myself, knowing full well that the pungent spices borrowed from India travel everywhere the Brits go. I so badly wanted to ask her for curry but decided not to. I told her I would have the fish and chips and the cottage pie along with a pint of Guinness stout. She winked at me and said, "K, love. Yuh mus be starvin," and walked to the kitchen.

A pint and a half of Guinness later, my food arrived. The waitress laid both dishes in front of me. The fish looked like regular fish and chips, except the batter on the fish was a bit more golden than usual. The fries were big, fat, odd wedges of potatoes with the skin on. The cottage pie resembled a shepherd's pie, with a crusty topping of potatoes covering the dish like a blanket.

I brought a piece of the fish to my mouth, and the aroma of red curry wafted through my nostrils like a tornado touching down. The tender pieces of mullet, which were meaty and flaky, were dredged with a seasoned flour of citrus flavors from the turmeric, heat from black peppercorns, and hints of warm nutty cumin—all the basic ingredients of a curry powder.

I plunged my fork into the thick, cloudlike golden-crusted potatoes and into my mouth. My palate continued to dance from the spices. The ground lamb mixture laced with curry powder married so well with the blanket of potatoes.

I devoured the hot food so quickly that my mouth, so cool from the chilled Guinness, sated the burning—a sweet burning.

TO COLOMBIA

URUGUAY

MONTEVIDEO PUNTA DEL ESTE

FROM FALKLAND ISLANDS

The name "Uruguay" comes from Guaraní, an indigenous language of South America. It is a versatile country with an impressively high standard of living compared to other South American countries: liberal laws, high literacy rate, excellent social services, and the best health-care system on the continent. Some say it's the French Riviera of South America. An influx of Europeans from the early 1500s through the late 1800s greatly influenced Uruguay's architecture and the culture of its major cities.

This tiny country, tucked away between Brazil and Argentina, is South America's second-smallest country. It's a land of rolling hills and verdant pampas, where cattle roam freely all year long, thanks to a moderate climate. The phenomenally gorgeous coastal region of Punta del Este is not only the hideaway for most of the country's urban middle class, it's also a popular destination for the continent's elite celebrities and dignitaries. And for the anthropologist in you, the lovely Colonia del Sacramento might be your cup of yerba maté, as it is Uruguay's oldest town and a UNESCO World Heritage Site.

As for its culinary delights, well, traditional European-type foods took root on the Uruguayan dinner plate. Pizza and pastas with savory sauces galore dress up Italian-influenced dishes. Local (German) pubs serve the best *cerveza*, and some of the best sausages, along with sauerkraut, are touted by street vendors. The Spanish and Portuguese left an indelible culinary imprint of sweet and luscious cakes and cookies, such as *alfajores*, which are shortbread cookies sandwiched together by exotic fruit jams and *dulce de leche* (caramel syrup). The favorite pastime of Uruguay's countrymen is undoubtedly soccer, which is served up with a juicy, charred grilled slab of *asado* (grilled beef) and a chilled pint of Patricia, an Uruguayan pride, brewed with wholesome locally grown barley.

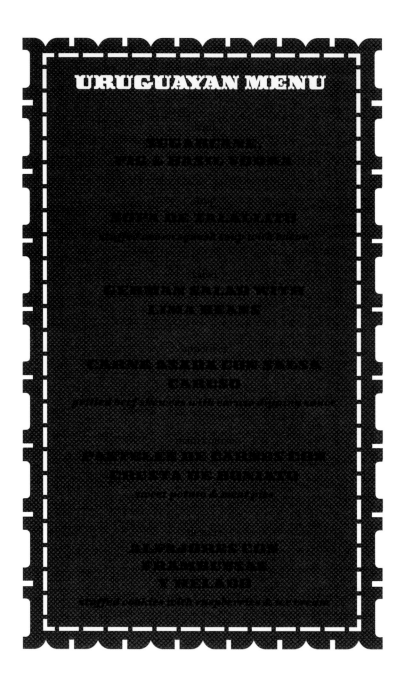

URUGUAYAN MENU

arrived in the quaint town of Colonia del Sacramento after a three-hour ferry ride from Buenos Aires. As soon as I arrived, I was greeted by a petite, curly-haired, olive-skinned woman who led me by the hand to her dilapidated blue automobile. She was a complete stranger. Her name was Lola, and she told me that I could stay with her and her daughters and that she would cook for me. Her rates were reasonable, and I wanted to spend two days in Colonia before I headed to Montevideo. Why not?

As she attempted to start her car, the engine struggled. I knew what was coming. She asked if I would push. I stepped out and pushed, and a puff of black smoke painted a black patch on my beige cargo pants. The engine struggled for life. *Put, put, put.*

I hopped inside the moving car and was greeted by a blast of furnace-hot air on my face. My lungs filled with exhaust fumes. About a half hour later, leaving a trail of dust and smoke in our wake, we arrived at her lovely home. The whitewashed veranda was laden with thick scarlet bougainvillea vines. Her two gorgeous daughters ran out to the dirt road with their scrawny brown dog chasing after them. Appearing shirtless on the veranda was her husband, a man with a beard down to his protruding belly. I instinctively knew that I was going to be fed very well.

For the next two days, my life was a true feast, with fig drinks, meat pies, sweet desserts, and other wonderful dishes.

SUGARCANE, FIG & BASIL VODKA

{ serves 2 }

Lola's husband made this vodka drink by squashing overripe figs, along with basil leaves, from their front yard. Figs and other fruit are plentiful in Uruguay. At practically every street corner, you'll find stands selling fresh local and organic fruits, plus some imported from Argentina and Brazil. You'll find canned sugarcane juice at Latin and West Indian markets.

2 small ripe figs, plus 1 cut into wedges for garnish (optional)

½ cup canned sugarcane juice

½ cup vodka

4 basil leaves, Thai or Italian, plus more for garnish

Ice

1. In a small pitcher, combine the 2 figs, sugarcane juice, vodka, and 4 basil leaves. Crush the mixture with a wooden pestle, the back of a wooden spoon, or a muddler.

2. Pour the mixutre through a strainer into a martini shaker, add ice, and shake vigorously.

3. Pour into 2 chilled martini glasses. Garnish with fresh basil leaves and a wedge of fig, if desired.

SOPA DE ZALALLITO

stuffed acorn squash soup with bacon

I had this wonderful soup at Lola's house. It was served to me in a hollowed-out round squash similar to acorn squash. I've also since tried it with a hybrid I found in California called eight-ball squash, which can be green or yellow and also tastes very similar to acorn squash.

2 round acorn squash (about the size of large grapefruits)

Extra-virgin olive oil for brushing, plus 1 tsp

Sea salt

Freshly ground black pepper

2 strips bacon, finely chopped

2 small shallots, thinly sliced

½ tsp ground annatto

1 tsp ground cumin

1½ cups low-sodium vegetable or chicken stock

½ cup canned unsweetened coconut milk

Two 3-inch-square pieces toast

2 oz shredded Monterey Jack cheese

2 tsp freshly grated Parmesan cheese

2 squash blossoms for garnish (optional)

1. Preheat the oven to 325°F.

2. Cut off the tops of the squash about 1 inch from the stem end and reserve. Scoop out the seeds and discard. Cut a very thin slice off the bottoms of each squash to create a stable base. Using a small paring knife, cut about ¼ inch of flesh from the perimeter of the insides of the top so that the opening is a bit wider. (Do *not* trim the outer skin of the squash or the lids will not have a snug fit.) Brush the insides of the squash and the flesh side of the lid with olive oil. Season with salt and pepper.

3. Arrange the squash bowls, with tops alongside, stem-ends up, in a large lightly greased baking pan. Bake for 30 minutes. Remove from the oven and set the pan with the squash aside. Increase the oven temperature to broil.

4. Meanwhile, in a saucepan, heat 1 tsp olive oil over medium-high heat. Add the bacon and cook until crisp. Reduce the heat to low, add the shallots, annatto, and cumin and cook for 1 minute, stirring constantly. Add the stock and coconut milk, and season with salt and pepper. Simmer for 8 to 10 minutes.

5. Ladle the hot soup into the squash; don't fill to the rim. Top each with the toast and sprinkle with the cheeses. Transfer to the broiler and cook until the cheese is bubbly and brown, about 3 minutes. Serve immediately, each topped with a lid and garnished with a squash blossom, if desired.

   NOTE Squash flesh shrinks during baking; if any holes form, still serve the soup in the squash halves but set them in soup bowls.

GERMAN SALAD WITH LIMA BEANS

{ serves 2 to 4 }

This tasty salad may be served warm or chilled. I first had it cold, which was a welcome treat in hot weather. The parboiled beans and hard-boiled eggs make this a hearty dish.

1 lb white russet potatoes, peeled and cut into 1-inch cubes

1 cup shelled fresh lima beans

Sea salt

1 Tbsp white wine vinegar

½ cup mayonnaise

¼ cup finely chopped celery

2 Tbsp thinly sliced green onion (green part only)

2 Tbsp sweet pickle relish

1 tsp Dijon mustard

2 Tbsp chopped fresh parsley

Freshly ground black pepper

2 hard-boiled eggs, peeled and chopped

½ cup pitted black olives

1 Cover the potatoes and lima beans with 2 inches of cold water in a large saucepan. Add a pinch of salt and bring to a boil over medium-high heat, then reduce the heat to medium, stirring once. Cook until the potatoes are tender, about 8 minutes.

2 Drain the potatoes and beans. In a large bowl, lightly toss the beans and potatoes with the vinegar and let it sit for 20 minutes.

3 Add the mayonnaise, celery, green onion, relish, mustard, and parsley and season with salt and pepper. Toss lightly.

4 Divide the salad among bowls and sprinkle with equal portions of eggs and olives. Serve warm or chilled.

I was in lovely Punta del Este looking for something comforting: a meal reminiscent of home. I was tired of feasting on meat and exotic fruits for the numerous months I'd been traveling in South America. I found a pizza joint, but the pizza tasted nothing like the pie I longed for from Gabby's, in Queens, New York.

A few miles down the beach, I came to a restaurant. Although the chalkboard announced the usual *asados* and *batidos* (fruit drinks), what stood out was German potato salad. One ingredient in this dish provides great comfort for me: potatoes. I can live on mashed potatoes for days.

I had seen German potato salad on menus in Colombia, Peru, and Argentina, and I had passed it by. But finally I succumbed to the salad that contained one of my favorite comfort ingredients. I was glad I had tried it.

CARNE ASADA CON SALSA CARUSO

{ serves 2 }

grilled beef skewers with caruso dipping sauce

If you traveled to Uruguay without tasting a savory piece of the local farm-raised beef, well, you'd be missing out. The beef tastes better because the cattle are grass-fed and bask in South America's sunshine and moderate temperatures all year long. Similar to a béchamel, the delicious thick white Caruso sauce—an Uruguayan creation named for an Italian opera singer—is also great with pasta and spooned over oysters or chicken breasts before baking.

1 lb beef tenderloin, cut into 1-inch cubes

½ cup apple juice

½ cup white wine

1 tsp minced garlic

1 tsp ground cumin

2 Tbsp minced fresh parsley

1 tsp freshly squeezed lime juice

2 Tbsp olive oil

CARUSO DIPPING SAUCE

2 Tbsp extra-virgin olive oil

1 small shallot, finely chopped

1½ tsp minced garlic

¼ cup white wine

One 4-oz can sliced mushrooms, drained

1 cup heavy cream

½ tsp cayenne pepper

1 Tbsp chunky peanut butter

Sea salt

Ground white pepper

☀ Thread the beef cubes onto two 12-to-14 inch metal skewers, dividing them evenly.

☀ Place the kebabs in a baking pan. In a small bowl, whisk together the apple juice, wine, garlic, cumin, parsley, lime juice, and olive oil. Pour the marinade over the kebabs, cover with plastic wrap, and refrigerator for at least 1 hour or up to overnight, turning occasionally so they marinate evenly.

☀ Build a hot fire in a charcoal grill or heat a gas grill until very hot.

☀ To make the dipping sauce: While the grill is heating, in small saucepan, heat the oil over medium heat. Sauté the shallot and garlic for 1 minute, add the wine and mushrooms, and cook for 3 minutes more, or until boiling.

☀ Add the cream, cayenne, and peanut butter. Reduce the heat to low and bring to a simmer. Cook for 3 minutes more. Season with salt and white pepper. Transfer the mixture to a blender and blend until smooth.

☀ Arrange the skewers on the hot grill. Grill the kebabs for 3 to 5 minutes on each side for medium-rare, or longer for well-done. Serve with Caruso dipping sauce.

PASTELES DE CARNES CON CRUSTA DE BONIATO

sweet potato & meat pies

Comfort food does not get any better than Lola's meat pie. But instead of using regular potatoes, she made it with white *boniatos* (also called *batatas*), similar to sweet potatoes, which complement this dish with a touch of sweetness and make it delicate and fluffy. Serve with a garden salad.

SWEET POTATO TOPPING

2½ lb peeled sweet potatoes, cut into 1-inch pieces

4 Tbsp unsalted butter

⅔ cup evaporated milk

⅓ cup whole milk

Sea salt

Ground white pepper

3 Tbsp extra-virgin olive oil

2 lb ground veal

1 large onion, finely diced

2 Tbsp chopped garlic

2 tsp chopped fresh thyme

Sea salt

2 tsp ground cumin

1 tsp cayenne pepper

2 Tbsp tomato paste

½ cup dry white wine

½ cup low-sodium chicken stock

4 celery stalks, cut into ½-inch-thick slices

Freshly ground black pepper

1. To make the topping: In a large saucepan, combine the potatoes and enough cold salted water to cover by 1 inch. Bring to a boil, uncovered, and cook until fork-tender, 15 to 20 minutes. Drain in a colander.

2. Force the potatoes through a ricer. Discard any tough fibers.

3. In the same saucepan over low heat, add the butter and both milks. Bring to a simmer and stir to melt butter. Using a whisk, slowly whisk in the potatoes. Increase the heat to high and stir constantly until the texture is thick like mashed potatoes, about 3 minutes.

4. Season with salt and white pepper. Remove from the heat and set aside.

5. Preheat the oven to 350°F.

✳ In a 2½-quart heavy cast-iron skillet over medium heat, heat the olive oil. Add the ground veal and cook, stirring frequently, until lightly brown, about 5 minutes. Add the onion, garlic, thyme, and a pinch of salt. Cook, stirring, for about 2 minutes more. Add the cumin, cayenne, and tomato paste and cook for 1 minute more. Add the wine, stock, and celery. Bring to a boil, stirring frequently, until all the liquid is absorbed, scraping up any brown bits. Season with salt and black pepper.

✳ Remove the skillet from the heat. Increase the oven temperature to broil.

✳ Spoon the sweet potato mixture over the cooked veal and spread evenly using a whisk, making a rough surface. Broil about 3 inches from the heat source until the top is golden, 3 to 5 minutes. Serve warm.

ALFAJORES CON FRAMBUESAS Y HELADO

stuffed cookies with raspberries & ice cream

The *alfajor* is a popular dessert throughout Uruguay. It's a shortbread cookie sandwich containing anything your sweet tooth might fancy. I prefer to use ice cream and raspberries. This recipe is tailored for the cooking students I teach in New York City public schools, so it makes a lot; store extra cookies in airtight jars and make however many sandwiches you want, whenever you want.

6 Tbsp butter, softened

1 cup superfine sugar

½ tsp freshly grated nutmeg

1½ tsp almond extract

2½ cups all-purpose flour, plus more for dusting

1 large egg

3 cups coffee ice cream, or your favorite flavor

½ pint fresh raspberries

1. Preheat the oven to 350°F. Have ready two nonstick baking sheets.

2. In a large bowl, combine the butter, sugar, nutmeg, and almond extract. Using an electric mixer, beat until smooth. Add the 2½ cups flour and the egg and mix until a smooth dough forms.

3. Shape the dough into a flat round disk. On a lightly floured surface, wrap it in plastic wrap and refrigerate for 45 minutes.

4. On a lightly floured surface, roll out the dough to a thickness of ¼ inch. Using a 2-inch cookie cutter, cut out 30 cookies, gathering dough scraps and rerolling as needed. Place the cookies on the baking sheets.

5. Bake until light golden, 10 to 12 minutes. Let cool completely before assembling ice-cream sandwiches.

6. Place 1 cookie upside down on a flat surface and scoop about 3 Tbsp of ice cream onto it, spreading smooth. Add a few raspberries and top ice cream with a second cookie, then smooth the sides. Place assembled ice-cream sandwich on a baking sheet in the freezer. Repeat with the remaining cookies, ice cream, and raspberries.

7. Freeze the ice-cream sandwiches, covered, for at least 1 hour, or up to overnight.

CARTAGENA

TO ECUADOR

BOGOTÀ

COLOMBIA

FROM URUGUAY

Nestled on the continent's northwest corner and surrounded by Peru, Venezuela, Brazil, and Panama, Colombia borders the Caribbean Sea and the Pacific Ocean. In 1819, Colombia became independent from Spain thanks to Simón Bolívar, the great liberator of his native Venezuela as well as Peru and Bolivia.

I won't lie: I went to Colombia for the food. The country is the world's largest exporter of plantains and grows the best coffee beans on Earth. Contributing greatly to this country's regional gastronomy is, no doubt, its diverse landscape and climate, which brings a bounty of fruits and vegetables. At high elevations on steep mountains, terrace-type farming allowed the indigenous Amerindians to grow a variety of crops, such as *maíze* (corn), squash, yucca, chiles, beans, quinoa, and cotton. Other culinary influences came from the Spanish and the Portuguese in the early fifteenth century; these Europeans brought sugarcane, coffee, cattle, and chickens.

Every region I visited had something unique to offer in both cuisine and landscape. On the country's northern tip, the city of Cartagena is a bustling hub and tourist hot spot. Here, the Caribbean coastline is dotted with pretty thatched-roof houses. Huge homes with bougainvillea-covered verandas and grand shady trees are nestled on quaint, narrow cobblestone streets that reminded me a bit of a picturesque scene from New Orleans.

Cartagena is renowned for its balance and harmony of flavors, clearly influences from the Caribbean. There's a wide variety of fish and shellfish. Two local dishes include coconut rice with raisins and, my favorite, shad fish stew with coconut milk.

The gorgeous capital of Bogotá is a fusion of old and new, from the magnificent old mansions and art galleries to the financial district's sophisticated skyscrapers. And on a clear day you can see the powdery white coats of the mountains in the distance. Street food in Bogotá varies. My favorite are the tamales, which are made with corn and either minced beef, pork, or chicken and wrapped in banana leaves. Other delicacies are *pan de yuca, pastel Gloría, roscónes,* spiced sausage, *chicharrónes,* and *aborrajados* (deep-fried plantains stuffed with cheese).

Colombia's mountains rise eloquently like giant staircases, forming spectacular verdant plateaus at different heights. These mountainous plateaus, found in a variety of climates, produce a mélange of ingredients, from coffee to flowers. I've had everything from fresh yucca bread to *buñuelos* (deep fried balls with cheese in the dough), to *arepas* (rather thick corn tortillas often made with cheese and served with butter) with scrambled eggs for breakfast.

To the east of the Andes lies more than half of Colombia's undeveloped territory. The Orinoco and Amazon regions with navigable rivers give a bounty of freshwater fish. Here, the natives use yucca to make drinks and breads. They also hunt for wild game, such as venison.

COLOMBIAN MENU

drink
REFANO
soda beer

salad
BAKED AVOCADO & CRABMEAT SALAD

appetizer
TAMALES DE POLLO Y PLÁTANOS DULCES
chicken & sweet plantain tamales

main course
STUFFED PORK LOIN WITH COCONUT MILK GRAVY

dessert
ESPRESSO CHOCOLATE CUPS

REFANO

soda beer

This drink, a mix of the local beer and the national soda, literally fizzed my palate. In Barichara, where I first imbibed this brew, Águila beer was used along with Colombiana soda, which tastes like Red Bull but with more fizz. If you cannot find Colombiana, I recommend cream soda.

1½ cups Columbiana brand soda or cream soda, well chilled

½ cup Águila beer or light beer, well chilled

¼ cup pineapple juice

2 pineapple wedges for garnish

In small pitcher, combine the soda, beer, and pineapple juice and lightly stir. Divide between 2 chilled beer mugs and garnish each with a pineapple wedge. Serve immediately.

Barichara is a town influenced by the Spanish and filled with old charm—narrow pathways and whitewashed stone churches. It's also where I met Enrique. In my hotel's bar, Enrique insisted on ordering for me a refreshing *refano* as well as a local delicacy called by the locals *la hormiga culona* (the big-butt ant).

I initially thought Enrique was pulling my leg, since I had divulged my love for the national soft drink, Colombiana. I had also had a similar drink in Chile called *calimocho*, which is mixed with red wine and soda. But the drink came, and it was delicious. As for my new culinary find, it hardly excited my palate. *La hormiga culona* is literally ants with big behinds that are pan-roasted and taste a lot like burned popcorn.

BAKED AVOCADO & CRABMEAT SALAD

{ serves 4 }

Avocados are abundant in Colombia, and in every market you can find heaps of them. At each home or street-food stall I visited, I feasted on some type of tasty salad made with avocados. The unique soil and climate of Colombia really has an effect on the texture and taste of fruits and vegetables. But since in America we grow some meaty avocados ourselves, you'll still be able to achieve the complex flavor.

8 oz jumbo lump crabmeat, picked through for cartilage

1 Tbsp freshly squeezed lime juice

1 small shallot, minced

1 tsp chopped fresh cilantro

1 Tbsp heavy cream or mayonnaise

Sea salt

Freshly ground black pepper

2 large, firm but ripe avocados, cut in half and pitted *(see note, page 104)*

2 oz shredded Monterey Jack or mozzarella cheese

2 Tbsp freshly grated Parmesan cheese

4 small lime twists for garnish

❉ Preheat the oven to 475°F. Lightly grease a medium baking pan.

❉ In a small bowl, combine the crabmeat, lime juice, shallot, cilantro, and cream. Lightly toss, and season with salt and pepper. Set aside.

❉ Cut a very thin slice off the rounded outer edge of the avocados to create a stable base. Place the avocado halves in the prepared baking pan, hollow-side up. Divide the crabmeat mixture evenly among the avocado hollows.

❉ Cover the surface of the avocados evenly with both cheeses. Transfer to the oven and bake until the cheese is bubbly and light brown, 3 to 5 minutes. Garnish each with a sprinkle of chives and a lime twist. Serve immediately.

As I passed through the Colombian countryside in a *chiva* (rural bus), I bought dozens and dozens of tamales. *Chivas* are the most colorful vehicles to grace rural Colombia; not even the most lavish stretch limos could take their place. The *chiva* made stops from village to village, and my spine would tingle as we rode by the lovely, winding roads hugging the sides of cliffs and valleys and lush, dark green hills.

I felt as if I were riding in something magical, with the wind blowing in my hair from every direction. The *chiva's* body is wood, and it is painted in the most shocking colors. You will find only the poor riding these vehicles. Our *chiva* picked up passengers who came aboard with chickens, bundles of yellow corn, freshly picked squash leaves, pigs, and everything else indispensable to the villagers and their way of life. When the *chiva* stopped for passengers, a sea of street vendors hawked their wares, from tamales to fragrant, ripe pineapples to colorful drinks.

BAKED AVOCADO & CRABMEAT SALAD

{ serves 4 }

Avocados are abundant in Colombia, and in every market you can find heaps of them. At each home or street-food stall I visited, I feasted on some type of tasty salad made with avocados. The unique soil and climate of Colombia really has an effect on the texture and taste of fruits and vegetables. But since in America we grow some meaty avocados ourselves, you'll still be able to achieve the complex flavor.

8 oz jumbo lump crabmeat, picked through for cartilage

1 Tbsp freshly squeezed lime juice

1 small shallot, minced

1 tsp chopped fresh cilantro

1 Tbsp heavy cream or mayonnaise

Sea salt

Freshly ground black pepper

2 large, firm but ripe avocados, cut in half and pitted (*see note, page 104*)

2 oz shredded Monterey Jack or mozzarella cheese

2 Tbsp freshly grated Parmesan cheese

4 small lime twists for garnish

Preheat the oven to 475°F. Lightly grease a medium baking pan.

In a small bowl, combine the crabmeat, lime juice, shallot, cilantro, and cream. Lightly toss, and season with salt and pepper. Set aside.

Cut a very thin slice off the rounded outer edge of the avocados to create a stable base. Place the avocado halves in the prepared baking pan, hollow-side up. Divide the crabmeat mixture evenly among the avocado hollows.

Cover the surface of the avocados evenly with both cheeses. Transfer to the oven and bake until the cheese is bubbly and light brown, 3 to 5 minutes. Garnish each with a sprinkle of chives and a lime twist. Serve immediately.

As I passed through the Colombian countryside in a *chiva* (rural bus), I bought dozens and dozens of tamales. *Chivas* are the most colorful vehicles to grace rural Colombia; not even the most lavish stretch limos could take their place. The *chiva* made stops from village to village, and my spine would tingle as we rode by the lovely, winding roads hugging the sides of cliffs and valleys and lush, dark green hills.

I felt as if I were riding in something magical, with the wind blowing in my hair from every direction. The *chiva's* body is wood, and it is painted in the most shocking colors. You will find only the poor riding these vehicles. Our *chiva* picked up passengers who came aboard with chickens, bundles of yellow corn, freshly picked squash leaves, pigs, and everything else indispensable to the villagers and their way of life. When the *chiva* stopped for passengers, a sea of street vendors hawked their wares, from tamales to fragrant, ripe pineapples to colorful drinks.

TAMALES DE POLLO Y PLÁTANOS DULCES

chicken & sweet plantain tamales

The tamales I had on my journey were magical; each country has its own varieties. Colombian tamales are made with cornmeal, stuffed with succulent shredded pork or juicy moist chicken, and wrapped with fragrant plantain leaves (I use banana leaves). I make lots of these so I can freeze and re-steam them when needed. You may want to warn uninvited guests that the husks and plaintains leaves are not edible. Serve with hot sauce.

1 lb boneless, skinless chicken breast, cut into 2-inch pieces

1 large ripe plantain, peeled and cut into ½-inch slices *(see page 101)*

Sea salt

¼ cup extra-virgin olive oil

2 tsp minced garlic

2 Tbsp minced shallot

1 Tbsp smoked paprika

1 tsp cayenne pepper

2 tsp ground cumin

2 Tbsp chopped fresh cilantro

Freshly ground black pepper

1 package banana leaves, about fifteen 6-inch squares aluminum foil, or 1 package corn husks

1. In a saucepan, combine the chicken and plantains and add enough cold water to cover by 2 inches. Add a pinch of salt and bring to a boil over medium-high heat. Reduce the heat to medium and cook until the plantains are fork-tender, 8 to 10 minutes.

2. Remove the chicken with a slotted spoon. When the chicken is cool enough to handle, shred into small pieces and set aside.

3. Remove the plantains with the slotted spoon and reserve the cooking liquid. Force the plantains through a ricer, discarding any tough fibers, and set aside.

4. In a saucepan over medium heat, heat the olive oil. Add the garlic, shallot, paprika, cayenne, and cumin. Cook for 2 minutes or until the shallots have softened.

5. Add the shredded chicken and mashed plantains and stir to coat with the oil and spices. Cook, stirring frequently, until the chicken and plantains are warmed through. Add ¼ cup reserved cooking liquid and cook over low heat until the liquid is absorbed, 3 to 4 minutes more. Add the cilantro and season with salt and pepper. Remove from the heat and set aside to cool.

✻ To assemble the tamales using banana leaves or aluminum foil: Place a banana leaf or a square of aluminum foil on a work surface and spoon about 3 Tbsp of the plantain mixture into the center of each leaf or square. Fold the top edge over the filling (toward you); then fold the bottom half up and over the filling (away from you). Now fold both remaining sides under to form a small packet and set aside. Repeat to assemble the remaining tamales. If using banana leaves, secure each parcel with butcher's twine or a strip of banana leaf.

✻ To assemble the tamales using corn husks: Soak the husks in a large bowl of warm water until softened and pliable, 3 to 4 hours. Separate the husks, trying not to tear them. Keep any husks that split; you can use two pieces as one by overlapping them or tear them into strips for ties (see below). Remove a corn husk from the water and pat dry. Lay the husk on a work surface, pointed end closest to you, and mound about 3 Tbsp filling in center. Flatten the filling slightly into a rough oval (about $\frac{1}{2}$ inch thick) with the back of a spoon, leaving a 1-inch border on both sides. Bring the pointed end of the husk up over the mound of filling to cover, and fold the sides of the husk over the filling to enclose. Gather together the open end of the husk at the top of the filling, creating a flat pouch, and tie with a corn-husk strip. Repeat to assemble remaining tamales.

✻ Arrange the tamales upright in rows in a steamer insert so that they resemble fallen dominoes. Set the steamer over boiling water in a large pot and cover with a clean folded kitchen towel or additional husks or banana leaves. Steam the tamales, tightly covered with a lid for about 10 minutes. Add more water as necessary. Using tongs, carefully remove the packets from the pot and let cool slightly. Serve the tamales warm in their husks or leaves.

STUFFED PORK LOIN
WITH COCONUT MILK GRAVY

I devoured this plateful of stuffed pork slices smothered in coconut milk, with a heap of rice on the side, while watching a cockfight in someone's backyard in the Andes. It was divine, especially since that night I ate with my hands—just like I did as a little girl. I love making this dish—and the best part is the leftovers.

1 large firm but ripe plantain

Sea salt

1 Tbsp extra-virgin olive oil

½ cup finely chopped chorizo or other spicy smoked sausage

1 large shallot, minced

1 Tbsp minced garlic

¼ cup chopped celery

1 tsp ground cumin

Fresh ground black pepper

2 lb pork loin

Coconut Milk Gravy
(facing page)

1. Peel the plantain (see note, page 101) and cut into 1-inch pieces. Transfer to a small saucepan and add enough cold water to cover by 1 inch. Add a pinch of salt and cook until fork-tender, about 4 minutes. Drain and chop finely. Set aside.

2. In a large, heavy, ovenproof skillet, heat the olive oil over medium heat. Add the chorizo and cook, stirring, until brown, about 2 minutes. Remove from the skillet and set aside in a small bowl.

3. Reduce the heat to low. Add the shallot, garlic, celery, and cumin and cook, stirring often, until tender, about 1 minute. Add the cooked plantain and chorizo and season with salt and pepper. Cook, stirring, for about 1 minute. Transfer the chorizo mixture to a bowl and set aside.

4. Let the skillet cool a bit, then wipe clean. Set aside.

5. Preheat the oven to 375°F.

6. Using a sharp knife, butterfly the pork loin about 2½ inches deep; make sure not to cut all the way through the loin. Season on both sides with salt and pepper. Spoon the plantain-and-chorizo mixture in between the two flaps of meat, fold the meat over the stuffing, and secure with butcher's twine.

7. Transfer the stuffed loin to the skillet and bake for 35 to 40 minutes. Remove the loin and let rest for 10 minutes.

8. Slice the pork loin, arrange on a serving platter, and serve drizzled with the Coconut Milk Gravy.

COCONUT MILK GRAVY

½ cup canned unsweetened coconut milk

1 tsp ground cumin

¼ cup low-sodium chicken or vegetable stock

1 Tbsp chopped fresh chives

1 Tbsp finely chopped fresh parsley

Sea salt

Freshly ground black pepper

In a small saucepan over medium-high heat, combine the coconut milk, cumin, stock, chives, and parsley. Bring to a boil, cooking until it thickens, about 2 minutes. Season with salt and pepper. Remove from the heat and set aside until ready to use.

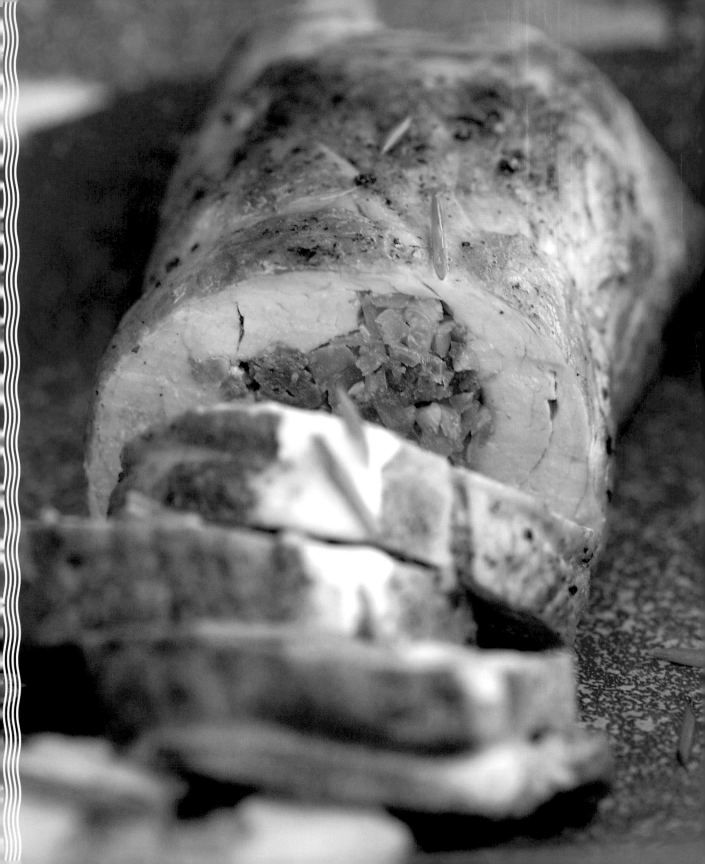

When I was in the Andean region, my driver, Hector, told me we were going to a cockfight arena. We had left Bogotá and stopped in the small town of Ibagué in the department, or state, of Tolima. I asked Hector if they had real beer in bottles and not "that yucca juice fermented with human saliva." For weeks, I'd been guzzling down yucca juice. Hector smiled and said that he had something special planned for me. We drove to a village. The evening sun was shimmering softly behind the mountains.

We entered the front yard of a small house, where the leaves of a deciduous tree had fallen on top of purple and white buttercup flowers set in flowerpots cut from car tires. In the backyard, the cockfight arena looked more like a chicken coop. Hector brought me a chilled Águila and excused himself. I guzzled the beer quickly with a manly thirst. The yard was packed with shirtless, charming men with olive complexions and watchful eyes. As they clutched their prized fighters to their open chests, they smiled at me and made flirtatious remarks in Spanish.

Hector came back with another Águila and something wrapped in plantain leaves. He opened the leaf to reveal the crisp brown pieces of skin from a suckling pig. One bite and the warm pig fat dissipated on my cool tongue, the crunch of crispy skin a taste of pure comfort food.

After the cockfight, and about six Águila beers later, it was time for the finale. Hector brought over a plateful of stuffed pork slices smothered in coconut milk with a heap of rice. It was divine.

I travel the world to bring back ingredients for my company, Nirmala's Kitchen. So, naturally, I have frequented plantations at far corners of the world. Getting to my destination is like a quest for gold, combing through jungles with my machete. On one such journey, my adventure led me to the department, or state, of Quindío, the coffee hub of Colombia. On this quest, I was sourcing coffee beans for one of my larger retailers. Once there, I was treated with the utmost hospitality by the plantation owners, but I chose to go home with the farmers who toiled the plantations. In most ways, they reminded me of my childhood in Guyana, as my parents were farmers.

Uncle Galeno, who worked in one of the coffee plantations, took me to meet his family and to have dinner at his home, which had a stunning view of a lush valley. He said he had the best coffee at home. He picked the beans himself. We hand-washed them, toasted them on a very rustic wood-burning brick stove, and ground them manually using a stone mortar and pestle. The experience was exhilarating, and the espresso he made for me was simply exquisite. And all this, while I looked over the endless valley of verdant coffee plantations.

ESPRESSO CHOCOLATE CUPS {serves 6}

After a delicious home-cooked dinner with plantation worker Galeno and his wife, Luisa, I was given the most decadent espresso custard. Made by the woman of the house, it was drizzled with *dulce de leche*. Into my mouth the custard went, with a velvety, volcanic burst of warm, buttery vapor dissipating onto my palate. That day, the sweet heat of the chile, the caffeine, and the luscious brown sugar had me quivering like a junkie. This is my version of that succulent dessert.

½ cup loosely packed brown sugar

¼ cup cornstarch

Sea salt

2½ cups whole milk

1 tsp ground cinnamon

⅛ tsp cayenne pepper

2 Tbsp instant espresso powder

6 oz bittersweet chocolate, coarsely chopped

1 tsp almond extract

Fresh mint leaves for garnish

☀ Combine the brown sugar, cornstarch, and a pinch of salt in the top of a double boiler. Slowly whisk in the milk. Add the cinnamon and cayenne, scraping the sides of the pan with a heatproof spatula to mix the dry ingredients.

☀ Place the pan over simmering water and stir occasionally with the whisk, scraping the bottom and sides.

☀ When the mixture begins to thicken and coats the back of the spoon, 25 to 30 minutes, add the espresso powder and chocolate. Continue whisking for 2 to 4 minutes, or until the pudding is smooth and thickened. Remove from the heat and stir in the almond extract.

☀ Pour mixture into 6 ramekins and refrigerate until firm and well chilled, 3 to 4 hours. When ready to serve, garnish with the mint leaves.

FROM COLOMBIA

 ESMERALDAS

QUITO

GUAYAQUIL

ECUADOR

TO BOLIVIA

About one thousand miles off Ecuador's coast, the Galapagos Islands drape the equator in the Pacific Ocean like a drenched, sleeping willow tree. Their dramatic, beautiful volcanic landscapes have some of the most unusual species of animals on Earth, including giant tortoises, sea lions, land and sea iguanas, fur seals, and many species of colorful birds. Anyone visiting the islands will undoubtedly be impressed with what the wildlife sanctuary has to offer.

Although Ecuador may be the smallest of the Andean countries, its regions and landscapes are as varied as its culinary table. Mainland Ecuador shares borders with Peru to the east and south, Colombia to the north, and the Pacific Ocean to the west. The Andean highlands run like a wide north-south backbone through the country's center, and their altitude dramatically diversifies the equatorial climate and vegetation, creating markets teeming with fresh and wholesome produce. Thanks to its climate and the variety of flora and fauna, this species-rich nation has something to stir the senses of everyone. It is the home of the original Panama hat and has no shortage of warm, friendly people. In fact, evidence that Ecuadorians are a spiritual people abounds—more so than in any other South American country I visited—from the uncanny rituals of the Incas to the formal liturgies of Catholicism introduced by the Spaniards, who first arrived from Peru in 1530. Ecuador gained its independence in 1822 from the Spanish, thanks to the famed South American liberator Simón Bolívar.

As for its cuisine, there is no significant foreign culinary influence in the Ecuadorian kitchen, except for Chinese takeout with its staple fried rice and noodle dishes. Remaining basically intact, Ecuador's cuisine embraces native ingredients with only a touch of Spanish influence.

The foods throughout Ecuador, from Esmeraldas to Quito to Guayaquil, vary widely. They include wild game, such as armadillos, guinea pigs, and monkeys. No part of an animal goes to waste. Delicacies such as *guatíta* (cow stomach, peanut sauce, and potatoes), *caldo de manguera* (pork intestines soup with rice), and *tronquito* (bull penis soup) are all delicious.

Other staples include potatoes, coffee, plantains, tomatoes, beans, and lots of seafood (for making tasty ceviche, including one version I had with black clams). Every meal I consumed was accompanied by rice and *ají* (chile sauce). I love rice and hot sauce; I can eat bowls of it and be a happy woman.

ECUADORIAN MENU

drink
NARANJILLA SPICED PUNCH

appetizer
LLAPINGACHOS RELLENOS
potato pancakes with ecuadorian peanut sauce

main course
BRAISED OXTAIL WITH CRANBERRIES

dessert
CARAWAY SEED COOKIES WITH DULCE DE LECHE

NARANJILLA SPICED PUNCH {serves 4}

Naranjilla, which tastes like bitter orange with a hint of peachy sweetness, is a delight to cook with. This wonderful fruit has smooth, bright yellow-orange skin and is the size of a plum tomato. In the United States you find them frozen; they are also available online and in Latin American stores. On the street in Esmeraldas, I had this punch with a dash of homemade *aguardiente*, which is made with sugarcane juice that's been fermented and distilled. At home in the States I like to use rum instead. Serve this for your friends in a giant punch bowl and they will love it.

4 cups apple cider

One 2-inch piece cinnamon stick

6 whole *naranjillas*, thawed and halved

Ice

½ cup dark rum

Slices of orange for garnish

In a medium saucepan over low heat, combine the cider, cinnamon stick, and *naranjillas*. Bring to a boil. Remove from the heat, cover, and let steep for 5 minutes. Strain into a pitcher filled with ice. Add the rum and stir. Ladle into punch glasses, garnish with oranges slices, and serve.

For the nature lover in me, there is no place like Ecuador. But when I reminisce about Ecuador, and the reason for my visit, nothing else comes to mind except José Santiago.

José, a frail but hard-working Ecuadorian immigrant, left behind his village and his family in 1993 to move to Queens, New York. Like many South Americans, José came to live the American dream, hardly keeping anything for himself and sending money back to his wife and children.

When I am in New York, I cook Ecuadorian meals for José. He calls out the recipes with the ingredients and I replicate his favorite dishes. It is challenging at times. One day, he asked for *tronquito*, a soup made with bull's penis. This is not my typical style of cooking, but, in the end, I persevered with the help of my local butcher. My heart wells up with joy to see José enjoying the Ecuadorian meals he misses so dearly. I am honored by the satisfaction in his blood-shot eyes and the delight and laughter that spreads across his face, which looks like a wrinkled newspaper as he shyly covers his toothless mouth.

LLAPINGACHOS RELLENOS

potato pancakes with ecuadorian peanut sauce

This is a wonderful vegetarian recipe that I learned from my mother and that I modified Ecuadorian style. It is a quick and simple dish to make, especially if you boil the potatoes with the skin on. Every type of food establishment in Ecuador carries this dish, from villagers' kitchens to street-food vendors to restaurants. The sauce is truly delicious; I use it over grilled chicken or pork and toss leftovers onto a salad.

3 large unpeeled potatoes
(*about 3 lb*), scrubbed

Sea salt

¼ cup finely chopped fresh
chives

½ tsp minced shallot

2 Tbsp finely chopped fresh
cilantro

Freshly ground black pepper

2 large eggs

1 tsp cayenne

1 tsp curry powder

Oil for frying

Ecuadorian Peanut Sauce
(*facing page*)

1. In a large saucepan, combine the potatoes and a large pinch of salt. Add enough cold water to cover by 1 inch. Bring to a boil over medium heat, cover, and cook until fork-tender, 18 to 20 minutes. Drain, cover, and refrigerate until well chilled. (The potatoes can be boiled 1 day ahead. Keep refrigerated.)

2. When ready to make the pancakes, peel the potatoes. Using a box grater, coarsely grate the chilled potatoes into a large bowl. Add the chives, shallot, and cilantro. Mix well and season with salt and pepper.

3. Meanwhile, in a small bowl, beat the eggs, cayenne, and curry powder. Gently fold into the potato mixture. Using your hands, form the mixture into 2½-inch-diameter pancakes about 1 inch thick. Lay them on a greased baking sheet. Cover with plastic wrap and refrigerate for at least 4 hours, or up to overnight.

4. In a heavy-bottomed 12-inch skillet over medium-high heat, heat 2 Tbsp oil until hot but not smoking. Working in batches, add potato pancakes and fry until golden brown, 6 to 8 minutes per side, adding more oil as needed. Drain on paper towel.

5. Serve warm with the peanut sauce.

ECUADORIAN PEANUT SAUCE

{ makes about 1½ cups }

2 Tbsp extra-virgin olive oil

2 large shallots, thinly sliced

1 cup whole milk

½ cup creamy peanut butter

1 tsp brown sugar

1 Tbsp chopped fresh cilantro

Sea salt

Freshly ground black pepper

In small saucepan, heat the olive oil over medium heat. Sauté the shallots until soft, about 1 minute. Reduce heat to low, add the milk, peanut butter, brown sugar, and cilantro and cook for 5 minutes more. The sauce should be slightly thickened. Season with salt and pepper. Set aside until ready to serve.

BRAISED OXTAIL WITH CRANBERRIES

{ serves 4 to 6 }

I shared this meal with my driver and his aunt, who made it as an offering for her deceased sister on All Soul's Day. As I sat in the dark shed outside their home, feeding myself with one hand and brushing away mosquitoes with the other, a touch of sweetness hit my palate from bits of the delicate, shredded oxtail meat. No doubt, this sweetness was an influence from the Moors, who once occupied Spain, by way of the Spanish settlers. Oxtail can be made into stew or soup. You can use different fruits, such as dates, prunes, quinces, or cranberries. Serve this stew with rice or crusty bread.

2 Tbsp extra-virgin olive oil

3 lb oxtail

Sea salt

1 medium yellow onion, chopped

2 Tbsp crushed garlic

1 tsp ground cardamom

1 tsp ground cumin

1 tsp red pepper flakes

Freshly ground black pepper

½ cup cherry or blackberry brandy

1 Tbsp grated orange zest

6 oz package dried sweetened cranberries

3½ cups low-sodium chicken stock

1. In a medium Dutch oven over medium-high heat, heat olive oil. Season the oxtail with salt, add to the pan, and brown the meat on both sides. Remove from the pan and set aside.

2. Reduce the heat to medium and add the onion, garlic, cardamom, cumin, red pepper flakes, black pepper, and a pinch of salt to pan. Cook, stirring constantly, until the onions are soft, about 2 minutes. Add the brandy, orange zest, and cranberries and cook for 2 minutes more.

3. Add the oxtail and stock and bring to a boil, then reduce the heat to low and simmer, covered, until the meat is tender and falling off the bone, about 1½ hours. Season with salt and pepper. Serve warm.

CARAWAY SEED COOKIES WITH DULCE DE LECHE

{ makes 20 to 25 cookies; 10 to 12 sandwiches }

The flavor of the caraway seed from Ecuador is more pungent than anise and dill with a fruity aftertaste, not like the North African types, which are milder. These cookies are divine alone or when drizzled with *dulce de leche*.

1¼ cups superfine sugar

7 Tbsp unsalted butter, softened

2 large egg yolks

1 tsp grated lemon zest

3 Tbsp freshly squeezed lemon juice

1 Tbsp whole caraway seeds

1¼ cups all-purpose flour

1 tsp baking soda

DULCE DE LECHE

One 14-oz can sweetened condensed milk

¼ tsp vanilla extract

¼ tsp freshly grated nutmeg

1. Cream the sugar and butter in a large bowl or cake mixer until light and fluffy. Add the egg yolks, lemon zest, lemon juice, and caraway seeds and mix until all the ingredients are well combined.

2. Sift the flour and baking soda into the butter mixture and stir until just combined. The dough will be quite soft.

3. Place the dough on a large piece of plastic wrap and form into a 1½-inch-diameter log. Twist the ends of the plastic securely, then place the dough in the freezer until hard.

4. Preheat the oven to 375°F. Line a baking sheet with parchment paper. Unwrap the dough and cut into ¼-inch slices. Place the cookies on the prepared baking sheet about 2 inches apart. Bake until just golden, about 12 minutes.

5. Allow the cookies to cool for 2 minutes on baking sheet, then slide them onto a wire rack and let cool completely. Store in an airtight container until ready to serve.

6. To make the *dulce de leche*: Preheat the oven to 425°F. Pour the condensed milk into an ovenproof pie dish, add the vanilla and nutmeg, and mix well. Cover with foil, place the dish in a hot water bath, and bake until the mixture thickens and begins to caramelize, about 2½ hours. Remove the foil and let cool. Refrigerate in a glass jar until ready to serve.

7. To assemble the cookies into sandwiches. Use a spatula to spread about 2 tsp of *dulce de leche* onto the flat (bottom) side of a cookie, then place another cookie on top.

FROM ECUADOR

 LA PAZ

B L V A

Named after Simón Bolívar, Bolivia is a land-locked Andean country. But don't let any geographical boundaries stifle your culinary imagination. It is a treasure trove of food, culture, and bewildering nature.

The country's unsurpassed beauty includes Salar de Uyuni, the world's largest salt flat, which is what drew me to this festive country in the first place—I was on a quest for gourmet salts for my company.

I felt as if I had just landed on a planet in outer space when I arrived at the Salar de Uyuni, a vast plain of dazzling whiteness stretching beyond the horizon. This terrain is primitive, yet unforgettable, an adobe of its own, dominated by the blistering sun, azure sky, and blinding white salt. Thousands of years ago, this was a high-altitude lake. Today, it has evaporated to dryness, but in the wet season it will carry a sheet of water on its surface of up to 3–6 inches.

Also complementing Bolivia's pristine beauty is Lake Titicaca. It is one of the most sacred places in the Incan Empire and still attracts thousands of religious devotees every year. Apart from being blessed with natural beauty, Bolivia possesses a large Amerindian population that has preserved its native languages and much of its traditional way of life, especially farming.

Bolivia, which gained its independence from the Spanish in 1825, borders Peru and Chile in the west, Brazil in the east, and Paraguay and Argentina in the south. The capital city, La Paz, sits at 12,792 feet, making it one of the highest cities in the world. On my first day, I felt as if I were back in Tibet, but when high-altitude sickness kicked in with pounding headaches, Bolivia had my remedy—coca leaf tea—which cured my altitude sickness in my travels to all the Andean countries.

Since Bolivia has different geographical zones, the country's climate, culture, and food vary. The landscape changes from the barren, high-plateau terrain of La Paz to the verdant plantations of bananas and coffee to the lush, tropical valley of Yungas in the foothills of the Andes.

In Bolivia, I found my gastronomic delight: pork, which brought back memories of my days in Indonesia and the Phillipines. Everywhere I visited, there was pork, from *lechón al horno* (roast-suckling pig) to *chicharrón* (cracklings) and *fritanga* (small pieces of fried greasy pork), too much of which could have put me in Heaven a little quicker. Although the street food in Bolivia differs by region, every meal is served with boiled potatoes or yucca, and sometimes both. Some traditional dishes include meat or vegetable *salteñas* (Bolivian empanadas), along with *locro,* a soup made with rice, quinoa, or fish. A favorite of mine is *humitas,* which are like tamales stuffed with cornmeal, cheese, and meat and steamed in corn husks or banana leaves. One adventurous meal I had was *charqui de llama,* which is dried llama meat cooked in corn and cheese.

❋ ❋ ❋

BOLIVIAN MENU

drink
CARICA YUNGUEÑO
papaya cocktail

soup
CONEJO DE CASTILLA
CON CEBADA
rabbit soup with barley

salad
SOLTERO DE QUESO DE CABRA
goat cheese salad with chayote

appetizer
JALLPAHUAICA
tamarillo salsa with yucca fries

main course
PAELLA LA VALENCIANA
quinoa with duck breast paella

dessert
HELADO DE OCA Y CANELA
purple & sweet potato ice cream

At the basin of the Amazon lies the Yungas, which means "warm lands" in indigenous Aymara, but don't let this word fool you. At night it gets really, really cold. My guide and driver, Domingo, brought me here so I could look for new ingredients for Nirmala's Kitchen and restock my supply of coca leaves.

I have developed a love for coca tea. I use it to make iced tea, which I sweeten with fresh sugarcane juice. The fresh-picked coca leaves remind me of the green tea leaves I picked in the Nilgiri tea plantation in India and in Japan. The flavor is very light and refreshing. I am an avid tea drinker, and I get almost a holistic feeling when sipping it warm or chilled.

The Yungas valley is abundant and lush, and produces the vast fruits and vegetables for the markets of the capital, La Paz. For days it had been pouring rain, and I enjoyed the sporadic white, ribbonlike waterfalls that draped the sides of cliffs in the green valley. The days were fragrant, filled with the smells of overripe guavas and something resembling freshly cut grass. At night, I smelled hints of *cumaru* wood and vanilla.

On my way to the valley, Domingo had me tasting nonalcoholic drinks, such as *chicha* (a very sour, rather bland drink made from fermented corn) and *tojorí* (also made from corn, sweetened and served thick and hot).

Frankly, none of these drinks was to my liking. Then Domingo introduced me to an alcoholic drink called *yungueño*. Made by the Amerindians in the Yungas valley, *yungueño* is mixed with a soda that tastes similar to 7-Up or Sprite, some sugar, and *singani*, a potent, uniquely Bolivian liquor distilled from Muscat grapes.

Domingo told me the locals, the majority of whom are Afro-Bolivian, have been drinking *yungueño* for as long as he could remember.

CARICA YUNGUEÑO

papaya cocktail

In the cool jungle of the Yungas at the base of the Amazon, I tried the regional cocktail known as *yungueño*. It was rather potent. To soften the taste of the main ingredient—*singani,* the national liquor, I did something unusual, at least by local standards: I added some mountain papaya, known as *carica,* that we had picked earlier that day. I thought it was quite delicious. The men in the village liked it, but said it was too fruity for them and decided to give it to the women.

10 to 15 fresh mint leaves, plus sprigs for garnish

¾ cup *carica* juice or papaya nectar

¼ cup pisco or white rum

1 tsp superfine sugar

2 thin lime slices

Crushed ice

Lemon-lime soda

In a small pitcher, combine the mint leaves, *carica* juice, pisco, sugar, and lime slices. Crush the mixture with a wooden pestle, the back of a wooden spoon, or a muddler. Pour through fine-mesh strainer, dividing the mixture evenly between 2 highball glasses. Fill each glass with crushed ice and top with the lemon-lime soda. Stir, garnish with mint sprigs, and serve.

CONEJO DE CASTILLA CON CEBADA

rabbit soup with barley

The Amerindian family I stayed with in the Yungas valley made this piping-hot hearty soup with *viscacha,* a wild animal that looks like a cross between a rabbit and a giant squirrel and is indigenous to the Andes. This versatile soup can be filled out with any wholesome goodness: leftovers, grains, root veggies, and other wild game such as iguanas and guinea pigs, or simply the all-too-celebrated chicken. Since we don't have *viscacha* roaming around the United States, I use rabbit. It's the same texture and flavor. Or, you can stick with chicken.

¼ cup extra-virgin olive oil

1 large onion, finely chopped

1 Tbsp chopped fresh garlic

2 celery stalks, finely chopped

Sea salt

1 tsp sweet paprika

1 Tbsp ground cumin

1 lb rabbit loin, cut into ¼-inch strips

¼ cup barley, washed, drained, and soaked overnight

4 cups low-sodium vegetable stock, plus more as needed

1 cup peeled and diced russet potatoes

Freshly ground black pepper

½ cup fresh baby spinach leaves

1. In a large saucepan, heat the olive oil over medium heat. Add the onion, garlic, celery, and a pinch of salt. Sauté until soft, stirring frequently, about 4 minutes. Add the paprika and cumin and cook for 2 minutes more.

2. Add the rabbit and cook for 3 minutes more, stirring frequently. Drain the barely. Add the stock and barley to pan and bring to a boil. Cover and cook until the barley is tender, 25 to 30 minutes.

3. Reduce the heat to low, add the potatoes, stir, and cover. Simmer until the potatoes are fork-tender, 10 to 15 minutes. Add more stock as needed for desired consistency.

4. Season with salt and pepper. Add the spinach leaves and cook for another minute. Remove from the heat and ladle into warm soup bowls. Serve hot.

SOLTERO DE QUESO DE CABRA

{ serves 4 to 6 }

goat cheese salad with chayote

The inspiration for this salad comes from a famous market in the city of Cochabamba. Mercado la Cancha is possibly the most chaotic market in South America, but I love it because it is not a tourist spot. It teems with life. I bought fresh goat cheese; a chayote; *jamón serrano* (country ham), which resembles prosciutto; and a rather strong herb called *quilquiña*, which is at least ten times more pungent than cilantro and marigold flowers.

10 oz fresh baby greens

2 medium chayotes, peeled, seeded, and diced

½ cup red or yellow cherry tomatoes, halved

1 small shallot, thinly sliced

1 small red bell pepper, stemmed, seeded, and julienned

¼ cup pitted black olives, roughly chopped

Minced fresh *quilquiña* or 2 tsp cilantro

DRESSING

½ cup extra-virgin olive oil

3 Tbsp red wine vinegar

1 tsp freshly squeezed lime juice

½ tsp ground cumin

2 Tbsp honey

Sea salt

Freshly ground black pepper

8 oz thinly sliced prosciutto

4 oz goat cheese, crumbled

1 In a large salad bowl, combine the baby greens, chayotes, tomatoes, shallot, bell pepper, olives, and *quilquiña*. Lightly toss and set aside.

2 To make the dressing: In a small bowl, whisk the olive oil, vinegar, lime juice, cumin, and honey. Season with salt and pepper. Pour over the salad and toss to coat.

3 Divide the salad among plates and top with slices of prosciutto and crumbled goat cheese. Refrigerate the salad for 10 to 15 minutes before serving.

Although Bolivia is a couple thousand miles from my beloved home, Guyana, I thought about my childhood experiences while traveling in this land-locked country. One of the reasons is because the yucca root was used by indigenous peoples throughout South America and is still in use today; it surprises me to have a shared heritage across such a distance. Here is one memory:

Hayari's yard was lined with sweet-smelling, ripe fruit trees, as if Payo (my grandfather) and I had entered into a perfume bottle. Hayari and his wife were Payo's Arawak patients. They had no children and could not climb fruit trees, so I climbed every fruit tree in their yard. I picked extra fruit so Hayari could sell it. I also made cherry and guava jams from the overripe fruit so he could eat it with bland yucca bread. Sometimes I spiced the jams. One time I used a long pepper from India, which Payo had in his medicine bag. It gave the sweet jam a hint of gingery, peppery bite, and Hayari loved it.

On one visit, we grated yucca and drained the juice to make *cassareep*, a brown molasses-like condiment made sweet with brown sugar and spices. We dried yucca mush in the sun, pounding it with a large wooden mortar and pestle, then spread it onto a round, clay griddle and baked it over his open fire pit. His yucca bread was made with yucca flour and rainwater. It was like stuffing a handful of starch in your mouth. My mother used the plain white yucca flour to thicken fish soup.

JALLPAHUAICA

tamarillo salsa with yucca fries

{ makes about 1½ cups salsa and }
{ about 30 yucca fries; serves 4 }

This salsa-like sauce is usually made with ripened red tomatoes, but it was served with roasted tamarillos in Mercado la Cancha. The tamarillo has been a staple in Andean country for hundreds of years. The delicious sauce is the perfect complement to fish and lamb dishes, especially when grilled. I also use this as a great substitute for cranberry sauce around Thanksgiving time.

TAMARILLO SALSA

1 lb whole tamarillos *(about 6)*

Sea salt

⅓ cup extra-virgin olive oil

1 large shallot, thinly sliced

1 tsp minced garlic

½ tsp red pepper flakes

2 tsp sugar

¼ cup chopped fresh cilantro

YUCCA FRIES

1 lb yucca, cut into 3-by-¾-inch pieces *(see note)*

Coarse sea salt

2 tsp sugar

Vegetable oil for frying

1 To make the salsa: In a medium saucepan, combine the tamarillos, with the stems on, and a pinch of salt. Add enough cold water by 1 inch. Bring to a boil over medium heat and cook for 5 minutes. Drain and let cool. Roughly chop and set aside.

2 In a medium saucepan over medium heat, heat the olive oil. Add the shallot, garlic, and red pepper flakes and sauté until soft, about 2 minutes. Add the tamarillos and sugar, cook for 2 minutes more, toss in the cilantro, and season with salt. Remove from the heat and allow to cool before serving.

3 To make the fries: Place the yucca in a medium saucepan, add 2 tsp salt, the sugar, and enough cold water to cover by 2 inches. Bring to a boil over medium heat and cook for 8 minutes. Drain. Transfer to a baking sheet lined with paper towels and lightly pat dry with more paper towels.

4 In a heavy skillet over medium-high heat, heat enough oil for deep-frying (about 3 inches) until a deep-fry thermometer reads 365°F.

5 Carefully drop about six yucca spears into the hot oil and fry, turning occasionally until golden brown on both sides, 5 to 8 minutes. Drain on paper towels and immediately sprinkle with sea salt. Repeat with remaining spears. Serve hot with salsa.

NOTE Yucca can be purchased frozen or fresh. If fresh, remove the tough skin, split it in half, and remove the fibrous vein. If frozen, remove the fibrous vein.

PAELLA LA VALENCIANA

{ serves 4 to 6 }

quinoa with duck breast paella

I love this dish because of my obsession with duck. This is exactly what I had in the Yungas valley, where it's called La Valenciana, after the region in Spain where paella was born. But in place of the rice used by the Spanish, the natives of Bolivia use their prized grain quinoa, which they've been cultivating for thousands of years.

1 Tbsp extra-virgin olive oil

1½ lb boneless, skin-on duck breasts, cut into ¼-inch strips

1 large white onion, chopped

2 Tbsp minced garlic

1 Tbsp minced fresh *quilquiña* or broad-leaf oregano

1 tsp ground cumin

1 tsp ground annatto

1 tsp cayenne pepper

2 Tbsp tomato paste

Sea salt

1½ cups quinoa, rinsed thoroughly and drained in a fine-mesh sieve

2½ cups low-sodium chicken or vegetable stock, plus more as needed

Freshly ground black pepper

½ cup fresh or thawed frozen green peas

1 small red bell pepper, seeded and julienned

¼ cup chopped fresh chives

1. In a large nonstick skillet, heat the olive oil over high heat. Add the duck and sauté until golden, about 8 minutes. Remove excess oil, leaving only 2 Tbsp in skillet. Add the onion and garlic and sauté 2 to 3 minutes more, or until soft. Add the *quilquiña,* cumin, annatto, cayenne, tomato paste, and a pinch of salt. Cook for 1 minute more.

2. Reduce the heat to very low. Add the quinoa, stirring constantly for 30 seconds. Add the stock and cook, covered, until quinoa is tender, 25 to 30 minutes. Stir every 10 minutes and add ⅓ cup more stock if pan seems dry. The quinoa is done when the spiral-like germ of the grain is visible. Season with salt and pepper.

3. Remove the cover, stir in the peas and bell pepper, and cook until the peas are warm and all the liquid is absorbed, about 5 minutes more.

4. Remove from the heat and sprinkle with the chives. Let sit for 5 minutes more before serving.

During my travels throughout South America, I sampled many root vegetables, most of which I had never seen before. One example is *oca*, which has been cultivated for millennia and has been an integral part of the diet and commerce of the high Andes regions. This sweet tuber, which is part of the potato family, is very distinctive, with a flavor somewhere between sweet potatoes and another South American root vegetable called *olluco*.

The closest thing to *oca* in the United States is the delicious purple potato, which tastes a lot like its Andean cousin and is a worthy substitute in the Purple & Sweet Potato Ice Cream recipe (page 180).

HELADO DE OCA Y CANELA

{ serves 4 to 6 }

purple & sweet potato ice cream

During my stay in the Yungas valley, I had a lukewarm pudding made with *oca* (an indigenous tuber), milk, sugar, and cinnamon. But in the steamy jungle, I longed for how it would taste chilled. So I created this recipe using both purple potatoes and sweet potatoes as a substitute for *oca*.

2 or 3 small purple potatoes (about ¾ lb)

1 small sweet potato (about ¾ lb), halved

2 cups half-and-half

1 cup whole milk

1 large egg yolk

1 vanilla bean, halved lengthwise, seeds scraped out and bean reserved

1 tsp grated orange zest

¼ tsp sea salt

½ cup firmly packed dark brown sugar

½ tsp ground ginger

⅛ tsp freshly grated nutmeg

½ tsp ground allspice

⅛ tsp ground cloves

4 to 6 wafer cones

Dulce de leche for drizzling (page 163, optional)

1. In a large saucepan, combine the purple and sweet potatoes and add enough cold water to cover by 1 inch. Bring to a boil over medium heat and cook until the potatoes are tender, 10 to 15 minutes. Test for doneness by inserting a skewer into a potato—it should go in easily. Drain the potatoes and transfer to a medium bowl to cool. When cool enough to handle, peel and coarsely chop, then set aside.

2. Meanwhile, in a medium saucepan, combine the half-and-half, milk, egg yolk, vanilla seeds and bean, orange zest, salt, and brown sugar and cook over medium heat, stirring until mixture thickens slightly and coats the back of a wooden spoon, about 10 minutes. Remove from the heat and strain. Discard the vanilla bean.

3. In a food processor, combine the cooked potatoes, ginger, nutmeg, allspice, cloves, and cream mixture. Process until smooth. Pour into a bowl and let cool.

4. Freeze the custard in an ice-cream maker according to manufacturer's instructions.

5. To serve, place a couple of scoops of ice cream in each wafer cone and drizzle with the *dulce de leche* (if desired).

FROM BOLIVIA

BUENOS AIRES

ARGENTINA

TO CHILE

I f you've typecast Argentina as only the land of tango and Eva Perón, think again. As with many of my travel expeditions around the globe, it's the food and everything that surrounds it that delivers humbling surprises. In this case, it's beef and Argentina's main cooking method: grilling. There is no better place to learn how to grill than in the verdant, flat, and fertile pampas, the northeast region shadowed by the Andes and home to the *gauchos,* or cowboys. There in the endless pastures, hundreds of Angus and Hereford cattle graze in the lush landscapes.

Argentina is the eighth-largest country in the world. Its elongated size caresses much of the southern part of South America. Geographical highlights include the massive Iguazú Falls, which border Brazil; the remote areas in southern Patagonia; the picturesque island city of Ushuaia, the doorstep of Antarctica; and the swanky metropolitan capital of Buenos Aires, a haven for fine cuisines.

Today, Argentina's cuisines are a mélange of dishes from its indigenous residents, who harvested corn, yucca, and wheat and hunted for fish, shellfish, and wild game for hundreds of years; Spanish settlers; and European immigrants who arrived in the 1800s, such as the Irish and Italians, many of whom live in quaint ethnic communities and speak their native tongues. Each culture adapted their unique practices in crafts, such as rearing sheep, goats, and cattle; creating pungent cheeses; and cultivating wineries, orchards, and olive groves.

Meat is eaten quite a bit here, so if you are a vegetarian, stay clear. *Churrascarías* are restaurants that serve grilled foods, and every part of the animal is grilled. If you order a *parrilla,* be very hungry. This multicourse meal typically includes grilled brains, or sweetbreads; sausages; kidneys; liver (my favorite); and, as the main course, a large, juicy grilled steak of the most tender, succulent meat you have ever encountered. Menus will also offer empanadas, seafood, or vegetables.

And to top off that heavy Argentine meal, you can always find foam-laden lattes drizzled with *dulce de leche.* The sugar and caffeine is sure to set you in the mood for the true Argentina finale: a night of sensuous tango, the nation's famous dance, which is the best way to shake off a full belly.

ARGENTINAN MENU

drink
LICUADO DE MORA
mora berry fruit shake

soup
WHITE BEANS, CRABMEAT, KALE & CHARDONNAY SOUP

salad
JICAMA, BLUE CHEESE & PASSION FRUIT SALAD

appetizer
EMPANADAS DE CHORIZO Y QUESO DE CABRA
chorizo & goat cheese pastry

main course
GRILLED VEAL CHOPS WITH JALAPEÑO & BUTTERNUT SQUASH GNOCCHI

dessert
MANGO CUSTARD WITH SUGAR WAFERS

LICUADO DE MORA

mora berry fruit shake

Mora berries are South America's version of blackberries. They are grown in abundance in Argentina's northern territory. As a matter of fact, many of the berries from this region are exported to the United States. A grower in Tucumán made this wonderful *licuado* (smoothie) for me, with fresh cow's milk and sweet honey from the valley. The preferred drink of Argentinean children, these shakes can be made with any seasonal fruits. In this version, I add a bit of morning brain food: bananas and yogurt.

1 ripe banana, peeled and sliced

1 cup frozen *mora* berries or blackberries, thawed

1 cup low-fat or nonfat yogurt

2 Tbsp honey

½ cup ice

Combine the banana, berries, yogurt, honey, and ice in a blender. Blend until smooth. Divide into 2 tall glasses and serve immediately.

This soup warms my soul whenever I think of how Felix, my guide, made it. I had traveled all the way into Patagonia with him to the town of Ushuaia, the gateway to Antarctica. Felix joked that I would freeze to death and that the penguins were going to feast on me if I didn't fatten myself with his hardy soup, made with a secret ingredient.

His secret ingredient turned out to be cheap white table wine, which I drank mostly to keep warm. The wine tasted awful by itself, but when he added it to the flavored broth, beans, and kale, it really transformed the taste and textures. In addition to the wine, Felix mixed in meat from a giant red spider crab, which is indigenous to the waters there.

WHITE BEANS, CRABMEAT, KALE & CHARDONNAY SOUP

{ serves 4 to 6 }

The wine in this recipe really pulls together all of the flavors of the ingredients in this unique soup nicely. Don't bother buying expensive wine; a cheap Chardonnay will work just fine.

2 Tbsp extra-virgin olive oil

1 medium onion, chopped

1 Tbsp minced garlic

1 tsp crushed dried thyme

Sea salt

¼ cup Chardonnay wine

4 cups lightly packed chopped kale

6 cups low-sodium chicken or vegetable stock, plus more if needed

One 15-oz can white beans (*cannellini beans*), drained and rinsed

1½ cups jumbo lump crabmeat (*about 8 oz*), picked through for cartilage

Freshly ground black pepper

4 to 6 red and yellow cherry tomatoes, halved, for garnish

1 In a large saucepan, heat the olive oil over medium heat. Add the onion, garlic, thyme, and a pinch of salt. Sauté until soft, stirring frequently, about 3 minutes. Add the wine and cook for 2 minutes more, stirring frequently.

2 Add the kale and cook until wilted, about 2 minutes more, stirring constantly. Add the stock and beans and bring to a boil. Reduce the heat to low. Cover and simmer for 5 minutes more. Add the crabmeat and cook for 2 minutes more.

3 Add more stock as needed for the desired consistency. Season with salt and pepper. Ladle into soup bowls and serve hot, garnished with the tomatoes.

JICAMA, BLUE CHEESE & PASSION FRUIT SALAD

{ serves 4 }

Now, I am not a salad person, but when I tasted this, I couldn't complain. The crisp but sweet jicama with the saltiness of the blue cheese and hints of passion fruit really hit the spot. It's the perfect light meal before hitting the dance floor, or, in my case, a *milonga* (tango dance club).

6 oz baby spinach leaves

1 cup crumbled blue cheese

2 small jicama, peeled and cut into 3-inch long matchsticks

¼ cup canned or bottled passion fruit juice

¼ cup extra-virgin olive oil

2 Tbsp white wine vinegar

1 tsp freshly squeezed lime juice

1 Tbsp honey

⅛ tsp ground cumin

⅛ tsp cayenne pepper

Sea salt

Freshly ground black pepper

1. In a large salad bowl, combine the spinach, blue cheese, and jicama. Toss lightly.

2. In a small bowl, whisk together the passion fruit juice, olive oil, vinegar, lime juice, honey, cumin, and cayenne.

3. Toss the salad with the dressing to coat. Divide among 4 salad plates and season with salt and pepper.

EMPANADAS DE CHORIZO Y QUESO DE CABRA

chorizo & goat cheese pastry

At the Fiesta del Queso (Cheese Festival), which takes place every year in the village of Tafí del Valle, one of the lovely street vendors gave me this combination of fresh goat cheese and *morcilla* (blood sausage, or black pudding) enfolded in the warm pillow of an empanada. Here at home, to replicate the same taste and textures with ease, I use store-bought phyllo dough pastry and chorizo, both readily available at every supermarket.

4 oz goat cheese, at room temperature

1 cup finely diced *morcilla* or chorizo sausage

1 Tbsp finely chopped fresh chives

Sea salt

Freshly ground black pepper

Eight 8½-by-13-inch sheets frozen phyllo, thawed

1. Preheat the oven to 400°F. Lightly grease a baking sheet and set aside.

2. In a small bowl, mash the goat cheese with the sausage, chives, and a pinch of salt and pepper. Set aside.

3. Working with one phyllo sheet at a time, unfold the phyllo on a work surface. Place 1 heaping Tbsp filling on the bottom half of the dough. Fold the bottom half of the dough over the filling with one hand while pushing the filling down with your other hand. Fold the sides inward, then continue to roll the dough away from you. Transfer the empanada to the prepared baking sheet. Repeat with the remaining phyllo and filling.

4. Bake until lightly browned, 6 to 8 minutes. Serve immediately.

GRILLED VEAL CHOPS WITH JALAPEÑO & BUTTERNUT SQUASH GNOCCHI

{ serves 2 }

Of all the grilled meats in Argentina, the veal chop is my favorite. It just melts in your mouth. I've re-created an entire meal I had in the pampas, including delicious, warm squash gnocchi. This is truly a hearty and satisfying dish. After this meal, you will want to sit with the remote in hand, just like I do after making it for myself.

GNOCCHI

1 lb butternut squash, seeded, quartered lengthwise, and cut crosswise into 1-inch pieces

White pepper

1⅓ cups all-purpose flour, plus more for dusting

1 small egg yolk, lightly beaten

Extra-virgin olive oil, for drizzling

2 bone-in veal rib chops (about 14 oz each)

Sea salt

Freshly ground black pepper

3 Tbsp canola oil

Chopped parsley, for garnish

1. To make the gnocchi: Preheat the oven to 375°F. Lightly grease a medium baking pan.

2. Using a fork, lightly poke the flesh of the squash. Put it in the prepared baking pan and bake until fork-tender, about 45 minutes. Turn off the oven and let the squash sit for 15 minutes. Remove from the oven and let cool slightly.

3. Using a small paring knife, gently remove the skin and transfer the squash to a medium bowl (this should yield 1 cup baked squash).

4. Add a pinch of white pepper and the 1⅓ cups flour and mix well. Slowly add the egg and knead until a soft dough forms.

5. Lightly flour your hands and scoop out 1 tsp dough into the palm of your hand to form a flat disk. Press lightly with a dinner fork to make grooves on one side. If the dough sticks to the fork, lightly flour the fork before pressing the gnocchi. Repeat to shape remaining dough. Arrange the gnocchi in a single layer on a floured baking sheet.

6. Bring a medium pot of salted water to a boil.

7. Preheat the oven to 400°F.

8. Season the veal chops on both sides with salt and pepper.

continued

193

JALAPEÑO SAUCE

2 Tbsp unsalted butter

1 Tbsp minced jalapeño

1 tsp minced shallot

1 Tbsp finely chopped
fresh cilantro

Sea salt

Freshly gorund black pepper

9. In a large, ovenproof skillet, heat the canola oil over high heat and sear the chops until nicely browned, about 3 minutes on each side. Transfer the pan with the chops to the oven and roast for about 6 minutes for medium-rare, turning only once.

10. Transfer to a serving platter and cover loosely with foil to keep warm.

11. Cook the gnocchi a few at time in the boiling water until they rise to the surface of the water. Transfer to a bowl and drizzle with a bit of olive oil to prevent from drying while you make the jalapeño sauce.

12. To make the jalapeño sauce: In a small pan over very low heat, melt the butter and sauté the jalapeño, shallot, and cilantro. Cook until just soft and the butter is foamy. Season with salt and pepper.

13. Toss the sauce over the cooked gnocchi and serve warm, with veal chops. Garnish with the parsely.

MANGO CUSTARD WITH SUGAR WAFERS

{ serves 6 }

Sugar wafers are a popular item throughout South America, and are dipped into all sorts of jams. I sampled this mango custard with wafers from a street vendor at a bus stop. The subtle flavor of the mangoes balances the sweetness of the wafers well in this heavenly, decadently delicious dessert.

3 large ripe mangoes *(about 3½ lb)*, peeled and sliced

1½ Tbsp unflavored gelatin

½ cup cold water

½ cup boiling hot water

¾ cup sugar

¾ cup canned evaporated milk

1 package (11 oz) sugar wafers

1. In a food processor, purée the mangoes until smooth. Set aside.

2. In a medium bowl, soften the gelatin in the cold water. Add the cup of boiling water and stir until the gelatin completely dissolves. Set aside to cool.

3. Add the sugar and milk to the cooled mixture, and mix thoroughly until the sugar dissolves. Add the mango pureé and mix until smooth, then strain into a separate bowl.

4. Evenly divide mixture among six 8-ounce ramekins. Refrigerate until the mango custards are set, about 8 hours or up to overnight. Serve with the wafers.

FROM ARGENTINA

TO BRAZIL

 SANTIAGO

TEMUCO

CHILE

C hile brings out my wild side. Out of all the South American countries, Chile's slender, snakelike shape gracing the western edge of South America has one of the most varied and extreme climates and geographies on the planet. Chile's breathtaking backsplash of jagged spires includes more than fifty active volcanic peaks and the impassable walls of the Andes Mountains. The country also boasts exquisite tropical beaches, towering waterfalls, and shimmering lakes. In the Pacific, there's mysterious Easter Island and infamous Robinson Crusoe Island, with unique wildlife, including the fur seal and the red hummingbird.

To the north, Chile has the parched Atacama Desert, one of the most inhospitable regions on Earth. Its days are blistering hot, and the nights are frigid. However, Chile's center, including its capital, Santiago, has green landscapes of forest, fruit orchards, and vineyards.

Chile's southern extremity is marked by Cape Horn, a treacherous headland surrounded by the almost continuously storm-tossed seas of the Drake Passage and the passable—but only through the foggy stillness—Strait of Magellan. Farther down toward the edge of the earth is the Antarctic, a magical place of eternal whiteness.

Chile was colonized by Spain in 1541 and declared its independence in 1818. Today it's populated predominantly by *mestizos* (people of mixed Spanish and Amerindian ancestry) with heritages including the indigenous Aymara and Mapuche peoples. However, there is also a minority population from what seems like every part of Europe.

Spanish is Chile's official language, although sometimes you wouldn't know it since the locals drop syllables and tend to speak as fast as bullet trains. Apart from the numerous spoken Amerindian dialects, there is also the Polynesian language of Rapa Nui on Easter Island.

The country's cuisine greatly reflects its topographical variety. Chile's coastline is dotted with fishing ports, which bless the country's kitchens with some of the most exotic shellfish on Earth. I have seen huge *erizos* (sea urchins), razor clams, and abalone. A popular soup I discovered is *caldillo de congrio,* made with potatoes, onions, conger eel, and tomatoes; it's divine and hearty.

My quest for more traditional meals led me to Temuco, the cultural center of the Mapuche Amerindians, the area's original inhabitants. They use coca leaves, potatoes, green beans, squash, corn, and horse meat in my favorite stew, *charquican.* They also make some of the best travel snacks: *charqui,* which is jerky made from llama, beef, or horse meat. The tasty, gamey, yet chewy horse jerk is really delicious. And the jerk made from llama tastes like beef.

Another favorite is *curanto,* a stew made of chicken, pork, lamb, beef, fish, shellfish, and potato. The standard Chilean meal is *lomo a lo pobre,* an enormous slab of beef topped with fried eggs nesting on yucca chips. The *parillada* is a barbecue whereby every organ of an animal is grilled to perfection.

Chile's cuisine, and, of course, its superb wines, are arguably its pride—aside from being the birthplace of poet Pablo Neruda and the country's 2006 election of its first woman president, Michelle Bachelet Jeria. As for the peripatetic traveler, Chile's landscape will not disappoint.

CHILEAN MENU

drink
COLA DE MONÒ
monkey's tail

soup
CAZUELA
chilean comfort soup

salad
ARTICHOKE HEART, POTATO & PINE NUT SALAD

appetizer
COMPLETOS
chilean-style hot dog

main course
PAN-SEARED HALIBUT WITH TOMATILLO PEBRE & QUINOA-STUFFED HEIRLOOM TOMATOES

dessert
AVOCADO & COCONUT MILK ICE CREAM

I had just crossed the Peruvian border and was waiting for my prearranged ride to my hotel in Arica. But since my bus had broken down several times on the way and arrived in town late, and my driver was nowhere in sight, I figured that my ride had gone back to the hotel.

Arica is not a popular tourist spot. It's more like a stopover for beach dwellers and border crossers from Bolivia, Peru, and Chile. It is a rugged town with mostly suspicious-looking men trying to offer me anything that is sellable and pleasurable. At that time of the night, it was empty and no place for a woman. The sounds of barking dogs echoed through the dead night. I was as cold as I was lonely.

After I called my hotel to inquire about my ride, I sat on the ground, on top of my backpack, near a bright-blue juice shack. I pulled my baseball cap over my eyes to protect them from a single naked lightbulb surrounded by a swarm of night bugs. The juice vendor acknowledged me with a smile and asked if I wanted to buy a *burro de leche* (donkey's milk, aka Chile's Viagra drink). I declined because I had had enough from various food stalls. All I needed was a warm bed.

The juice vendor may have seen the tiredness in my eyes, or the shivering of my lips, because he pulled out his personal thermos and offered me a drink. The steam escaped as he poured the dark-brown liquid into the beaten-up silver thermos cap. The sight warmed my soul. A sip from the thermos cap revealed a hint of cinnamon, a rare but delightful ingredient on my travels in the interiors. The hint of heat from pink peppercorn hit the back of my palate, sending me into a heavy cough.

He called it *cola de mono* (monkey's tail). At first I thought it was *muday,* a drink made from fermented "monkey puzzle nuts" that I had had in the jungles. The juice vendor attempted to add *aguardiente,* a potent liquor, but I made the excuse of having altitude sickness. Instead, he added a few crushed coca leaves and let them steep for a bit before my next sip. At that point, I did not care when my driver arrived. The loneliness and longing for the easy comforts of my bed dissipated like a lump of sugar in tea.

COLA DE MONÒ

monkey's tail

I was given this warm drink while waiting outside a bus stop in the port town of Arica at three in the morning. There was nothing memorable about that night except this special elixir made with coffee, milk, chili, cinnamon, sugar, and liquor.

6 cups whole milk

2 Tbsp instant espresso powder or coffee

½ tsp ground cinnamon

½ tsp freshly grated nutmeg

1 Tbsp sugar

6 oz white chocolate, broken into small pieces

¼ cup Cointreau

4 small red Thai chiles *(optional)*

Whipped cream, for serving

Ground cinnamon for sprinkling

1 In a medium saucepan over medium heat, combine the milk, espresso, cinnamon, nutmeg, and sugar. Whisk well and bring to a boil.

2 Remove from the heat. Whisk in the chocolate and Cointreau to mix well. Add the chiles (if using) and let steep, covered, for 1 minute, then remove the chiles and reserve.

3 Pour into 4 mugs. Top each with a spoonful of whipped cream and a sprinkling of ground cinnamon. Garnish each mug with a reserved chile (if using) and serve immediately.

CAZUELA

chilean comfort soup

This Spanish-influenced Chilean soup is delicious and hearty. The primary ingredients are quinoa, chicken, chayote, and squash. I am omitting the chayote and using butternut squash because I just love them. You can use wild or regular rice if you don't have quinoa. Serve it with a crusty French baguette or slices of panettone.

¼ cup extra-virgin olive oil

1 large onion, diced

1 Tbsp chopped garlic

Sea salt

1 tsp crushed dried thyme

1 tsp red pepper flakes

1 Tbsp ground cumin

1 Tbsp tomato paste

1 lb boneless, skinless chicken breast, cut into ¼-inch strips

4 cups low-sodium vegetable stock

1 cup cooked quinoa *(see note, page 53)*

2 cups *(about 1½ lb)* ½-inch-dice peeled butternut squash

Freshly ground black pepper

¼ cup chopped fresh cilantro

1. In a large saucepan, heat the olive oil over medium heat. Add the onion, garlic, and a pinch of salt. Sauté until soft, stirring frequently, about 4 minutes. Add the thyme, red pepper flakes, cumin, and tomato paste anvd cook for 2 minutes more.

2. Add the chicken and cook for 3 minutes more, stirring frequently. Add the stock and bring to a boil. Cover and cook for 8 minutes more.

3. Reduce the heat to a low simmer. Add the cooked quinoa and butternut squash, stir, and cover. Simmer until the squash is fork-tender, 8 to 10 minutes.

4. Season with salt and pepper. Add the cilantro and cook for another minute. Remove from the heat and ladle into warm soup bowls. Serve hot.

ARTICHOKE HEART, POTATO & PINE NUT SALAD

{ serves 2 }

This truly is a hearty salad, and I often savor it as a full meal by adding purple or sweet potatoes. Chile has some of the meatiest artichokes I've ever tasted, and that's why they're the inspiration for this salad. The mustard gives it a nice bite. This salad can be made ahead of time and refrigerated.

1 lb red-skinned potatoes, unpeeled, scrubbed and cut into 1-inch pieces

Sea salt

¼ cup extra-virgin olive oil

1 Tbsp Dijon mustard

1 small red jalapeño, seeded and finely chopped

⅛ tsp cayenne pepper

1 Tbsp white wine vinegar

3 Tbsp chopped fresh mint

One 14-oz can artichoke hearts, drained and halved

Freshly ground black pepper

¼ cup pine nuts

1. Place the potatoes in a medium saucepan. Add a pinch of salt and cover with cold water by 1 inch. Bring to a boil over medium heat and cook until tender, about 10 minutes. Test for doneness by inserting a skewer into—it should go in easily. Drain and set aside.

2. In a medium bowl, whisk together the olive oil, mustard, jalapeño, cayenne, vinegar, and mint. Add the artichokes and cooked potatoes and lightly toss. Season with salt and pepper.

3. Divide the salad between 2 salad plates, and sprinkle with the pine nuts, and serve.

COMPLETOS

chilean-style hot dog

The very posh city of Viña del Mar, Chile's most luxurious resort town, attracts an eclectic mix of visitors from all over the world. Near Viña del Mar's soft stretches of white, sandy beaches there are many fancy gourmet restaurants, from which I detoured right to street food and discovered *completos,* Chile's answer to hot dogs. They are *muy grande* and stuffed with avocados, mayonnaise, tomatoes, and sauerkraut. Oh, did I forget to mention that they taste better with a chilled *cerveza?*

Two ¼-lb all-beef hot dog or sausage

1 Tbsp extra-virgin olive oil

1 Tbsp chopped fresh cilantro

1 medium jalapeño, stemmed and thinly sliced

1 small shallot, thinly sliced

1 Tbsp freshly squeezed lime juice

½ cup peeled and diced red or green tomatoes

1 large ripe avocado, halved, pitted, and flesh scooped from skin, roughly chopped *(see note, page 104)*

Sea salt

Freshly ground pepper

2 Tbsp butter, softened

½ tsp minced garlic

Two 6- to 8-inch sub rolls

1. Cook the hot dogs according to package instructions.

2. Meanwhile, in a bowl, whisk together the olive oil, cilantro, jalapeño, shallot, and lime juice. Fold in the tomatoes and avocado, lightly toss, season with salt and pepper and set aside.

3. In a small bowl, mix the butter and garlic. Spread the mixture onto the sub rolls. In a large frying pan over medium heat, place the rolls buttered-side down and toast until lightly golden.

4. To serve, tuck the hot dogs in the toasted rolls and top with the tomato and avocado mixture. Serve immediately.

PAN-SEARED HALIBUT WITH TOMATILLO PEBRE & QUINOA-STUFFED HEIRLOOM TOMATOES

This is truly a rustic dish; in many South American kitchens, the pantry is not always well stocked, so folks make do with what they have. And the taste isn't compromised one bit. It's a satisfying comfort meal, and the sauce and the quinoa can both be made ahead of time.

STUFFED TOMATOES

4 firm medium heirloom tomatoes *(2 to 3 lb)*

5 Tbsp extra-virgin olive, plus more for brushing

Sea salt

1 medium onion, finely chopped

2 tsp minced garlic

1½ cups cooked quinoa *(see note, page 53)*

⅓ cup chopped fresh cilantro

⅓ cup chopped fresh chives

Freshly ground black pepper

Four 6-oz skinless halibut fillets, bones removed

Sea salt

Freshly ground black pepper

1. To make the stuffed tomatoes: Preheat the oven to 375°F.

2. Cut a very thin slice off the bottom of each tomato so they will sit upright in the dish. Using a knife, score the bottom center of each tomato to form a cone that can easily be removed once the tomato is baked.

3. Place the tomatoes, stem-side up, in a pie dish, brush with olive oil, and sprinkle with sea salt. Roast just to soften, about 8 minutes.

4. Remove and let cool slightly, then spoon out and discard the centers to make room for the stuffing. Set aside.

5. In a sauce pan, heat 3 Tbsp of the oil over medium heat. Add the onion and garlic and sauté until soft, about 5 minutes. Add the cooked quinoa, cilantro, and chives and season with salt and pepper. Remove from the heat.

6. Spoon the quinoa mixture into the tomatoes. Set aside and keep warm or serve at room temperature.

7. Reduce the oven temperature to 225°F.

8. In a large, ovenproof skillet, heat the remaining 2 Tbsp olive oil over high heat. Coat the pan evenly until the oil is almost smoking. Season the halibut fillets with salt and pepper and place them in the skillet. Sear until golden brown, about 4 minutes. Turn the fillets and place the skillet in the oven. Bake until opaque throughout, about 15 minutes.

TOMATILLO PEBRE

¼ cup extra-virgin olive oil

1 tsp minced garlic

1 cup diced onion

1 medium jalapeño, stemmed and chopped

1 lb green tomatillos, husks and waxy coating removed, finely chopped

¼ cup chopped fresh cilantro

1 tsp freshly squeezed lime juice

Sea salt

Freshly ground black pepper

To make the *pebre:* In a medium saucepan, heat the oil over low heat. Add the garlic, onion, and jalapeño and cook until soft, stirring frequently, about 5 minutes. Add the tomatillos and cook until the juices thicken slightly, 10 to 15 minutes. Add the cilantro and lime juice and season with salt and pepper.

Remove from the heat and transfer the mixture to a food processor or blender. Blend until smooth. Adjust the seasoning with pepper.

Place a fillet on each of 4 plates and arrange stuffed tomatoes next to them. Spoon the *pebre* over the fish and serve immediately.

MAKE-AHEAD TIP Both the sauce and the quinoa can be made ahead and stored in the refrigerator.

My friend Felix and I flew to Easter Island, a long two-thousand-mile journey from mainland Chile. Under his arm, Felix caressed a box of avocados as if they were delicate eggs. He was taking them for his cousin who worked at one of the few quaint, one-story hotels on the island. Once situated on our first evening, we made a batch of avocado ice cream and feasted on bowls of it while watching the canopy of stars and listening to Felix's take on the history of the island.

It truly is a breathtaking island. For centuries, this UNESCO World Heritage Site had been isolated from the outside world. The people of Easter Island, or Rapa Nui ("Navel of Earth"), therefore developed their own distinctive culture, perhaps best known by their *moai* (huge figures carved of volcanic rock). Today, they still speak the Rapa Nui language.

AVOCADO & COCONUT MILK ICE CREAM

{ serves 6 }

Avocado ice cream is quite common in South American countries where the creamy green fruit is grown. South Americans tend to make ice cream with seasonal fresh fruits, and avocados are enlisted for their sweet side. This recipe incorporates some powdered vitamin C, as it keeps the color green as vibrant as if you had just sliced open an avocado.

1½ cups canned unsweetened coconut milk

2 ripe California avocados *(about 1¼ lb)*, **halved, pitted, and flesh scooped from skin** *(see note, page 53)*

½ cup sugar

One 500 mg Vitamin C tablet or Emergen-C pack *(see note)*

½ cup sweetened condensed milk

1 tsp vanilla extract

2 tsp freshly squeezed lime juice

1 tsp grated lime zest

1. In a blender, combine the coconut milk, avocados, sugar, and vitamin C tablet and blend until smooth and there are no visible lumps. Add the condensed milk, vanilla, and lime juice.

2. Pour the mixture into a large airtight container and fold in the lime zest.

3. If using an ice-cream maker, freeze the mixture according to manufacture's instructions before serving.

4. If you do not have an ice-cream maker, pour the mixture into a container and freeze until set, about 8 hours or overnight. Remove the ice cream from the container and cut into 3-inch pieces. Place in a food processor and process until smooth. Return to the airtight container and freeze again. Repeat the freezing and chopping process 2 or 3 times until a smooth consistency is reached.

MAKE-AHEAD TIP The ice cream can be made up to 1 week ahead and frozen in an airtight container.

NOTE Emergen-C packet can be found at any drugstore.

BRAZIL

RIO DE JANEIRO

TO PARAGUAY

FROM CHILE

Brazilians are fiercely passionate about their culture, cuisine, traditions, futbol (aka soccer), and, perhaps their greatest pride, the grandest party on Earth, Carnaval.

The world's fifth-largest country also boasts the largest river: the majestic Amazon. Brazil provides a rain-forest canopy sheltering the richest, most diverse ecosystem on the planet. With a massive concentration of flora and fauna, including millions of undiscovered plant and animal species, Brazil is a hotbed for nature lovers.

Just like its landscape, Brazilian cuisine is a kaleidoscope of unique ingredients, including numerous exotic fish and wild game from the illustrious Amazon and a bounty of vegetables and fruits, such as *guarana, açaí* berries, cacao, hearts of palm, passion fruit, yucca, and corn, just to name a few. With these ingredients, the native Amerindians thrived for hundreds of years, making fermented beverages, porridges, and breads.

The culinary influences of Brazil morphed with the arrival of the Portuguese in the 1500s. They brought with them a mélange of ingredients, including sugarcane. Today none of my Brazilian meals is complete without a *caipirinha,* the national drink made with *cachaça,* a clear spirit derived from sugarcane juice—unlike rum, which is made with molasses. Influenced by the Moors of North Africa, the Portuguese also brought to Brazil codfish, sardines, dried fruits, and lavish sugar-laden pastries and other sweets made with egg yolks.

In the 1600s, the slow demise of the Amerindians, who worked the sugar plantations, prompted the Portuguese to look for another source of labor, so they brought slaves from West Africa to Brazil. Some of the female slaves were sold to plantation owners to toil in their kitchens as cooks. In these kitchens, the slaves incorporated indigenous ingredients, like corn and beans with those brought from Portugal, such as garlic, salt, lemon, and chicken, and their homelands in Africa: okra, peanuts, bananas, and *dendê* oil (palm oil). One such fusion is *quindim,* one of my favorite desserts made with grated coconut and many eggs.

In the cosmopolitan cities, you will find the popular *churrasco,* a feast of grilled meats of all kinds. In some restaurants, the grilled meat is served *rodízio* style, meaning brought to your table on skewers and sliced by waiters while you wait. On almost every Brazilian table you'll find white rice and black beans, served with either steak, chicken, or fish. Additionally, no meal is complete without *farofa* (cassava meal) sprinkled over food and a generous dash of a favorite of mine, *malagueta* chiles, small round chiles steeped in *dendê* oil for that lovely yellow color and with a sweet heat that hits the back of your palate.

This predominately Catholic, Portuguese-speaking nation is a fusion of customs and rituals from various parts of the world; all have blended into a new culture that is uniquely Brazil. Each meal is like a feast, and when I visit Brazil, I feel like I'm in the backyard of my home country, Guyana, which sits right above it. I am transported to my childhood as I walk the streets of Rio or roam through rural villages in the Amazon region. I see reflections of my own self in the barefoot children selling delectable morsels as I did. Seeing bowls of exotic fruits in the scintillating Amazonian sun, I am at home in Brazil.

BRAZILIAN MENU

drink
CAIPIRINHA

soup
FEIJOADA BRASILEIRA
brazilian black bean stew

salad
BLACK-EYED PEAS & MANGO SALAD

appetizer
CRISPY POLENTA CHICKEN FINGERS WITH COCONUT MILK & CHEESE DIPPING SAUCE

main course
AUNTIE NEVIS'S BRAZILIAN HOLIDAY TURKEY DINNER:

cachaça & blood orange baked turkey

yucca & linguiça stuffing

garlicky kale

brazilian rice

dessert
PASSION FRUIT JELLIES

CAIPIRINHA

{ serves 1 }

In the pretty coastal town of Paraty, I drank *cachaça* in many forms—and it becomes a *caipirinha* with the recipe that follows. If you substitute the same amount of vodka for *cachaça,* the drink is called a *caipirosca.* And if you mix it with white rum, it's called a *caipiríssima.* Of course, for me, life is a little sweeter with vodka.

2 juicy limes, cut into ½-inch pieces, plus a wedge for garnish

1 Tbsp superfine sugar

4 oz cachaça, white rum, or vodka

Crushed ice

1. In a small pitcher, combine the lime slices and sugar. Crush with a wooden pestle, the back of a wooden spoon, or a muddler. Add the *cachaça* and mix well.

2. Strain the mixture in an old-fashioned glass and fill the glass with crushed ice. Stir, garnish with the lime wedge, and serve.

The *caipirinha* is Brazil's national drink, and there is no better place to savor this potent elixir than in the lovely colonial city of Paraty, which is about 140 miles southwest from Rio de Janeiro. In August, the city hosts the Pinga Festival, which celebrates the beloved clear spirit *cachaça,* which is made from sugarcane juice, rather than from molasses as rum is. The Paraty region is famous for producing this liquor.

In addition to making *caipirinhas, cachaça* is also used to make another famous Brazilian drink, the *batida.* To make a *batida,* Brazilians add *cachaça* to fruit juices, such as passion fruit, coconut, or papaya, with crushed ice and sugar. I think every home I visited gave me a different version of a *batida* before dinner, but after a couple of these drinks I couldn't remember if I even had dinner.

I first had *feijoada* in Sete Portas Mercado in the city of Salvador, in the state of Bahia. There it is made with wholesome black beans and many different smoked and sun-dried meats, especially pork and linguiça sausages. Then a few weeks later, I devoured this stew in the city of Manaus, which is the gateway to the Amazon. There I had a more adventurous version made with *guy* (guinea pig). In Guyana, my dad hunted these animals, which I grew up eating in soups and curries. This wild game is delicious, tastes like rabbit, and is indigenous to several South American countries.

FEIJOADA BRASILEIRA

{ serves 6 to 8 }

brazilian black bean stew

I've modified this elaborate Portuguese-inspired stew with popular and readily available ingredients—but I still keep it traditional. Serve it as a first course soup with crusty bread, or a main course with the customary accompaniments: side dishes of Garlicky Kale (page 233) and Brazilian Rice (page 234), or steamed white rice garnished with orange slices.

1 lb dried black beans, sorted and rinsed

4 Tbsp extra-virgin olive oil

4 strips bacon, halved

½ lb *linguiça* or kielbasa sausage, cut into 1-inch pieces

2 lb pork neck with bones, cut into 4- to 5-inch pieces

1 lb boneless beef short ribs, cut into 3-inch pieces

5 cloves garlic, peeled and smashed, plus 2 Tbsp minced garlic

5 bay leaves

10 cups low-sodium chicken or beef stock

1 small red onion, finely chopped

1 Tbsp tomato paste

NOTE If you want to make this into a soup, add more stock for the desired consistency.

1 In a large bowl, combine the beans and enough cold water to cover by 2 inches. Let soak overnight. Drain and set aside.

2 In a large Dutch oven over high heat, heat 2 Tbsp of the olive oil until hot but not smoking. Working in batches, brown the bacon, sausage, pork, and short ribs, turning occasionally, 3 to 4 minutes per batch. Transfer the browned meat to a large bowl, cover, and set aside.

3 Reduce the heat to low. Add the garlic cloves and bay leaves to the pot and stir constantly for 1 minute. Add the drained beans and 6 cups of the stock. Bring to a boil, reduce the heat to a simmer, and cook, uncovered, for 45 minutes, stirring occasionally and skimming the top.

4 Increase the heat to high, add the browned meats and remaining 4 cups of stock, and bring to a boil. Reduce the heat to low and simmer until the meat is falling apart, about 2 hours.

5 With a slotted spoon, remove about ½ cup of the cooked black beans from the pot. Using the back of a wooden spoon, slightly mash the beans and set aside.

6 In a small pan over medium heat, heat the remaining 2 Tbsp olive oil and sauté the onion and minced garlic until the onion is soft. Add the tomato paste and the smashed black beans. Cook for about 1 minute and transfer to the pot with the meat. Remove the bay leaves, stir, and cook for 5 minutes more. Serve hot.

BLACK-EYED PEAS & MANGO SALAD

There is something very special about a salad that's this earthy and sweet yet light. It goes well with a glass of chilled iced tea.

2 Tbsp extra-virgin olive oil

1 Tbsp balsamic vinegar

1 small shallot, thinly sliced

½ tsp ground cumin

2 Tbsp finely chopped cilantro

1 small red jalapeño, stemmed, seeded, and finely diced

Sea salt

Freshly ground black pepper

One 14-oz can black-eyed peas, drained and rinsed

2 large ripe mangoes, peeled and diced

1. In a medium bowl, whisk together the olive oil, vinegar, shallot, cumin, cilantro, and jalapeño. Season with salt and pepper.

2. Add the black-eyed peas and mangoes. Lightly toss and season with more salt and pepper. Cover with plastic wrap and refrigerate, up to overnight, until ready to serve.

CRISPY POLENTA CHICKEN FINGERS WITH COCONUT MILK & CHEESE DIPPING SAUCE

{ serves 4 }

My favorite street food in São Paulo is *frango con polenta* (fried chicken with polenta), which is the inspiration for this dish. The chicken is coated with cornmeal or polenta (or *angu,* as the locals call it), then fried. The white sauce is used for dipping like ketchup. The flavor of the sauce is very unusual for our American palate, but it's very tasty and simple to make. In the afternoon, the school children line up at street vendors for this after-school snack.

1½ lb boneless chicken breast

2 egg whites, lightly beaten

¾ cup ground polenta or cornmeal

Vegetable oil for frying

Sea salt

Freshly ground black pepper

COCONUT MILK & CHEESE DIPPING SAUCE

One 14-oz can unsweetened coconut milk

6 oz grated Parmesan cheese

1 Tbsp finely chopped fresh cilantro

1 Tbsp finely chopped fresh chives

Sea salt

Freshly ground black pepper

1. Pat the chicken dry on paper towels. Cut lengthwise into 1-by-3-inch strips. Dip the chicken strips in the egg whites and dredge in the polenta to coat. Lay on a baking sheet.

2. In a deep, heavy-bottomed pot over medium-high heat, heat enough vegetable oil for deep-frying (about 3 inches) until a deep-fry thermometer reads 365°F.

3. Fry the chicken in small batches until light brown, 3 to 4 minutes. Transfer to a wire rack and allow to drain. Season with salt and pepper and cover to keep warm.

4. To make the dipping sauce: In a medium nonstick saucepan over medium heat, bring the coconut milk to a boil. Slowly whisk in the cheese, then reduce the heat to low and continue to whisk until the mixture is reduced and is very thick, about 3 minutes. Add the cilantro and chives, whisking for another minute. Season with salt and pepper.

5. Transfer the cheese sauce to dipping bowls and serve immediately with the chicken fingers.

Christmas for us South Americans tends to be a downright feast. As a child in Guyana, I would graze our goats for weeks to fatten them in time for the holidays, when they would be slaughtered. On Christmas morning, I would see their lifeless bodies with heads dangling from the main limb of our guava tree. With their two-inch penknives in hand, my brothers would gleefully skin the goats. We would then make curried goat with all the trimmings. This was our Christmas tradition, year after year. We never had a whole turkey, although we had dreamed of one.

My Auntie Nevis, a petite, fair-skinned Portuguese woman from Brazil, would visit us a few times a year. During every Christmas dinner, she would try to detour our taste buds toward a roasted turkey by describing its flavor, its chest plump and glistening brown from baking in an oven.

As my brothers and I licked our curry-stained fingers from the goat, I wondered how something like an oven could make the turkey brown. It was difficult to imagine this without electricity. All I knew about baking stemmed from a mud oven smoothed over with cow dung.

Years later, I visited my very old and fragile Auntie Nevis in Brazil, and she gave me her roasted turkey recipe. She also showed me her gas oven (as if I had never seen one by then—I think she must've forgotten that I now live in the United States), but I let her indulge herself. I savored the moment, reminiscing about my childhood.

As she gracefully pointed to the beaten-up black knobs of her oven, the printed temperature numbers scrubbed off, she told me how to marinate the turkey with *cachaça*. She recounted how to prepare all the trimmings, too, including using ingredients I had cooked with as a child.

AUNTIE NEVIS'S BRAZILIAN HOLIDAY TURKEY DINNER

{ serves 8 to 10 }

With a few health-conscious adjustments, this is Auntie Nevis's traditional Brazilian holiday feast recipe. We omitted *dendê* oil, which is filled with saturated fat, and replaced the *farofa* with fresh yucca. I've also skipped the *malagueta* hot sauce, since it is too spicy, replacing it with Tamarillo Salsa (page 177), which has a taste similar to cranberry sauce. Other than that, it's pretty much how Auntie Nevis has made it for decades. Now my friends and family enjoy coming to my house for the holidays.

continued

CACHAÇA & BLOOD ORANGE BAKED TURKEY

MARINADE

2 cups cachaça or light rum

1 large white onion, diced

8 cloves garlic, chopped

1 cup tomato juice or V8 vegetable juice

1 cup extra-virgin olive oil

1 Tbsp finely chopped fresh thyme

1 cup freshly squeezed blood orange juice or regular orange juice

¼ cup grated orange zest

2 cups low-sodium chicken stock

One 12- to 14-lb turkey (*preferably kosher*), any feathers, quills, neck, and giblets removed

1 large plastic roasting bag

Sea salt

Freshly ground black pepper

6 Tbsp butter; 2 Tbsp softened butter, 4 Tbsp melted

1. To make marinade: In a large bowl, combine all the marinade ingredients and mix well.

2. Place the turkey inside a roasting bag and transfer to a large roasting pan.

3. Carefully pour the marinade into the roasting bag and then carefully remove all air pockets. Marinate the turkey overnight in the refrigerator.

4. When ready to bake the turkey, preheat the oven to 425°F.

5. Remove the marinated turkey from the plastic bag, reserving the marinade. Pat the turkey dry with paper towels. Sprinkle the turkey cavity with salt and pepper and brush the outside with the 2 Tbsp softened butter. Tie the legs together loosely to hold shape. Tuck the wing tips under.

6. Return the turkey to the large roasting pan and roast in the middle of the oven for 15 minutes. Reduce the oven temperature to 350°F.

7. Brush the melted butter over the turkey and roast, basting every 30 minutes (add a little water to pan if needed). Bake for 1½ hours.

8. Meanwhile, in a small saucepan over high heat, cook the reserved marinade until reduced by half. Strain and place near oven for basting.

CACHAÇA GRAVY

4 cups cachaça basting liquid *(reserved from turkey pan as needed)*

Chicken stock

¼ cup minced shallots

¼ cup all-purpose flour

1 tsp chopped fresh thyme

Sea salt

Freshly ground black peppar

Tamarillo Salsa *(page 177)* for serving

Fresh parsley for garnish

Blood orange for garnish

9. After 1½ hours, begin basting the turkey with the reduced marinade and continue to bake until a thermometer inserted into the center of the body cavity registers 165°F (fleshy part of thigh will be about 180°F; do not touch bone), 1 to 1¾ hours more. (Note: The total cooking time to bake this turkey is 2¾ to 3½ hours.) If the marinade starts browning too much, tent the turkey with foil.

10. Remove the turkey from the oven. Transfer to a carving board and let rest for 30 minutes.

11. To make the gravy: Pour the basting liquid from the turkey pan into a large measuring cup. Spoon off the fat from the top of the liquid measuring cup, reserving 2 Tbsp. You should have about 4 cups of basting liquid; if not, add chicken stock to equal 4 cups.

12. Heat 2 Tbsp of the reserved fat in a large saucepan over medium-high heat. Add the shallots and sauté for 1 minute. Reduce the heat to medium. Add the flour and whisk until golden, about 4 minutes. Whisk in the 4 cups basting liquid. Bring to a boil, continuing to whisk. Cook to desired consistency, about 5 minutes. Whisk in the fresh thyme. Season with salt and pepper.

13. To serve, carve the turkey and serve with the Tamarillo Salsa and gravy. Garnish the platter with the fresh parsley and slices of blood orange.

continued

YUCCA & LINGUIÇA STUFFING

You can use potatoes instead of yucca. To increase the serving portions, simply double the ingredients.

⅓ cup extra-virgin olive oil

½ lb *linguiça* or kielbasa sausage, cut into ¼-inch pieces

1 large Spanish onion, chopped

4 garlic cloves, finely chopped

3 lb cooked yucca, cut into ½-inch dice cubes *(see note)*

⅓ cup chopped fresh chives

Sea salt

Freshly ground black pepper

1 In a large saucepan, heat the olive oil over medium-high heat. Add the sausage and cook, stirring frequently until brown, about 3 minutes. Add the onion and garlic and cook for 3 minutes more, stirring frequently.

2 Remove from the heat. Add the yucca and chives and lightly toss. Season with salt and pepper before serving.

NOTE To cook yucca, peel the brown skin and split in half lengthwise. Core the long stringy fibers down the middle. Boil in salted water for 30 minutes or until fork-tender. Drain and allow to cool slightly before handling.

GARLICKY KALE

You can use collard greens instead of kale. To increase the serving portions simply double the ingredients.

10 cups packed kale *(about 2 lb)*, center ribs and stems removed, leaves coarsely chopped

¼ cup extra-virgin olive oil

6 garlic cloves, thinly sliced

1 large onion, finely chopped

1 tsp ground cumin

Sea salt

Freshly ground black pepper

1 In a large stockpot over medium high heat, cook the kale in boiling salted water until wilted, about 5 minutes. Drain in a colander.

2 In a large heavy skillet over medium heat, heat the oil. Add the garlic and cook until light brown, about 1 minute. Add the onion and sauté until soft, about 5 minutes.

3 Add the cumin and a pinch of salt, stir, then add the kale and sauté until heated through, about 4 minutes. Season with salt and pepper. Serve warm.

continued

BRAZILIAN RICE

I love rice, and this recipe is similar to what my grandfather made for lunch every single day in Guyana. I would not be surprised if Auntie Nevis learned this recipe from him, except hers has tomatoes; its all just delicious.

1 cup dried pigeon peas, soaked for 4 hours or overnight

⅓ cup extra-virgin olive oil

1 large white onion, finely chopped

2 Tbsp minced garlic

1 cup seeded and chopped tomatoes

Sea salt

4½ cups low-sodium chicken stock

1 cup parboiled rice

1 cup canned unsweetened coconut milk

2 Tbsp finely chopped green onion (green part only)

Freshly ground black pepper

1 Drain the pigeon peas and set aside.

2 In a large pot, heat the olive oil over medium-high heat. Add the onion, garlic, tomatoes, and 1 tsp of salt. Cook until the onions are softened, about 2 minutes.

3 Add the stock and drained peas and bring to a boil. Reduce the heat to medium and cook, uncovered, until the peas are nearly tender, about 15 minutes.

4 Reduce the heat to low and add the rice and coconut milk. Simmer, covered, until the rice is tender, about 20 minutes more. Stir occasionally.

5 Turn off the heat, add the green onion, and season with salt and pepper. Stir and allow to steam in the pot, covered, for 5 minutes more. Serve warm.

PASSION FRUIT JELLIES

{ serves 4 to 6 }

This recipe turns one of my favorite Brazilian ingredients, passion fruit, into one of my favorite American desserts, Jell-O. You can substitute the passion fruit for mango or peach.

4 cups chilled passion fruit juice

4 envelopes (4 Tbsp) unflavored gelatin powder

¼ cup sugar

Seeds of 1 fresh passion fruit for garnish

Whipped cream for garnish

1. Place 1 cup of the passion fruit juice in a large bowl. Sprinkle with the gelatin powder, stir, and set aside for 2 minutes.

2. In a small saucepan, combine the remaining 3 cups passion fruit juice and the sugar. Bring to a boil and stir to dissolve the sugar. Pour the juice into the bowl with the gelatin mixture. Stir until the gelatin completely dissolves, about 4 minutes.

3. Pour the mixture into glass serving dishes and refrigerate until set, 2 to 3 hours or up to overnight.

4. Garnish with fresh passion fruit seeds and whipped cream before serving.

FROM BRAZIL

PARAGUAY

ASUNCIÓN

Paraguay is nestled in the heart of South America between Brazil, Argentina, and Bolivia. For more than twenty years, Paraguay has had to be closed to tourism for political reasons. Asunción, the capital and largest city, is in the eastern region, where a large percentage of the population lives. In Asunción, the remnants of numerous coups and wars are still visible, but what dominates its landscapes are its colonial architecture, historic museums, shady plazas, a pink Congressional Palace, and the ruins of Jesuit settlements in the outskirts of Trinidad. Outside of Asunción, the pace of life is slow.

The Chaco region is one of the most pristine wildlife habitats left in South America. This savanna is vast, virtually flat, and sparsely populated with scrubs and forests. With its abundant and diverse plant and animal life, it's easy to feel like you're on a safari—South American–style. The unique variety of fauna includes jaguars, pumas, giant anteaters, and tapirs.

Paraguay's winding rivers are very navigable, and the wondrous Río Paraguay joins the Paraná and the Río de la Plata to give Paraguay an outlet to the sea. These rivers are filled with an abundance of fish, such as corvina, *pacú*, dorado, and the firm, tasty *surubí*. Paraguay's rivers are the nation's breadbasket because they transport goods to all parts of the country.

Paraguayans are extremely humble and would gladly break bread with anyone. The country's population is predominantly *mestizo*, a mix of European and mostly Guaraní ancestry, and Paraguayan cuisine incorporates many traditional cooking styles from this group. The influence of Paraguay's neighbors is evident in two of its popular meals: the *asados,* or *parilladas* (grilled beef), and empanadas. Other authentic, comforting favorites sold by street-food vendors are *chipas* (cheese cornbread), *soo-yosopy* (cornmeal and beef soup), and something very close to home for me, *albondigas* (meatballs).

PARAGUAYAN MENU

drink
TERERÉ
yerba maté–spiced tisane

soup
BORI-BORI
paraguayan hearts of palm soup

appetizer
EMPANADAS
RÍO PARAGUAY–STYLE

main course
CORNMEAL-ENCRUSTED
BAKED CATFISH

side dish
ROASTED TAMARILLOS &
PURPLE POTATOES

I was on a gaudy blue bus headed for Asunción. My head reverberated from the pothole-laden road and the bus's symphony of choking exhausts and squeaks resonating from the exposed rusty spring coils in half-torn seat cushions. My butt was numb from bobbing up and down. After a few hours of seesaw driving, the driver made yet another stop. A Guaraní girl of about ten in a blue frock came aboard. The girl, who had a round, sunburned face, was carrying a woven straw basket filled with leafy vegetables that looked like mustard greens.

Following her was her mother, who was meticulously balancing a huge, round basket on her head. The basket was filled with yellow-, brown-, and black-feathered baby chicks clucking wildly like a gang of loud-mouthed school children. In the woman's right hand was a huge brown burlap bag. The woman placed the girl's basket onto the empty seat adjacent to me. I smiled and nodded to her as she stood there looking for an okay from me.

I looked at the greens, salivating. At that moment, I wished for a pan, some shallots, hot chiles, olive oil, and some fire. I dreamed of sautéed greens and a bowl of rice. After a little while, the girl sat next to me, making an exchange with the basket of greens. I gave her the other side of my ear buds and we both listened to Nina Simone. We passed the fields of green crops from horizon to horizon, wild birds in pastures, and horse carts laden with lumber and hay. We stopped a few times for cow traffic.

A tug on my arm woke me from a miserable attempt at sleep. My back ached and my neck was stiff. The woman smiled at me as she held out a gourd elaborately designed with silver borders around the rim. The aroma from the gourd was *tereré* (yerba maté) with a hint of lemongrass. It was fused with other herbs as well. I brought the *bombilla* (straw) to my dusty, parched lips. The cool liquid streamed down my parched throat. It was my elixir of life—a heavy dose of caffeine.

The little girl who had been sleeping against me woke up, and I shared the *bombilla* with her. Sharing yerba maté and drinking from the same straw is a sign of friendship in several countries of South America.

TERERÉ

{ serves 4 }

yerba maté-spiced tisane

For many, yerba maté is an acquired taste. Called *tereré* in Paraguay, it's an herb whose leaves and stems, and sometimes roots, are used to make the strong beverage. It tastes like a fusion of *matcha* green tea, woodsy roots, and dried old thyme. In Paraguay, it's served hot or cold. You can find yerba maté tisane or tea bags in many gourmet food stores across the United States. In the summer, I brew it in my coffeemaker to produce large quantities. I serve it with freshly squeezed limes, honey, and ice to enhance the otherwise bland taste. For a delightful cocktail, I like to add vodka, a touch of orange juice, and some club soda.

2 cups water

1 star anise

2 cups filtered apple juice

3 yerba maté tea bags

Ice

Sugar

Fresh mint for garnish

1. In a large saucepan over medium heat, combine the water, star anise, and apple juice and bring to a simmer.

2. Remove from the heat and add the tea bags. Steep for 4 to 6 minutes, then remove the tea bags and star anise. Let cool to room temperature, then refrigerate until chilled.

3. When ready to serve, pour into 4 ice-filled glasses and sweeten with sugar to taste. Garnish with the mint leaves.

On the same sweaty, bumpy bus ride to Asunción, during which I sipped the cool and refreshing *tereré*, I also sampled a delicious soup.

The Guaraní woman, who was sitting in front on me, handed her daughter, who was sitting next to me, a red clay bowl with a wooden spoon. The girl looked at me with mesmerizing black eyes and spooned out *bori-bori*. She reached a spoonful of the warm soup to my lips before I had a chance to politely motion my hand to say no. I looked at her mother, who smiled and nodded her head to go ahead. The soup was divine.

It had small pieces of hearts of palm with just the right amount of salt and some big pieces of black pepper. There were white pieces of meat and a few tiny bones. "Must be pork," I thought. But it was too tender, so I figured it could have been rabbit . . . but then again it was a bit gamey. I stopped wondering what I was eating; the experience of this Guaraní girl feeding me superseded all other thoughts of what poor rodent-like animal I had just consumed.

BORI-BORI

{ serves 4–6 {

paraguayan hearts of palm soup

I enjoy making this soup on the weekends. When I come home from work on weekdays, I simply reheat it. In fact, it's so irresistible, I sometimes have chilled spoonfuls of it directly from the refrigerator at two o'clock in the morning.

2 Tbsp extra-virgin olive oil

2 small shallots, thinly sliced

2 Tbsp minced garlic

1 tsp ground cumin

1½ cups russet potatoes, peeled and cut into ¼-inch dice

4½ cups chicken stock, plus more as needed.

One 14-oz can hearts of palm, drained and finely chopped

1 cup canned unsweetened coconut milk

2 Tbsp chopped fresh cilantro

Sea salt

Freshly ground black pepper

Cayenne pepper for garnish

1. In a large saucepan, heat the olive oil over medium-high heat. Add the shallots, garlic, and cumin and sauté until the shallots are tender, about 2 minutes. Add the potatoes and the 4½ cups stock and bring to a boil, cooking for 8 minutes more. Add the hearts of palm and coconut milk and simmer on low heat for another 8 minutes.

2. Transfer the soup to a food processor or blender and purée. Add enough stock to thin to desired consistency. Return the soup to the saucepan and bring to a low simmer. Add the cilantro.

3. Season with salt and pepper. Ladle into bowls and garnish with a sprinkle of cayenne. Serve warm.

Captain Serg was fixing the oil-slicked engine on his boat. The moment I laid eyes on him, I thought, "WOW!" He was vast in every way. His tan, golden, hairless, beefcake chest was firm and glistening with beads of sweat from the radiant sun. His Zeus-like physique made his deckhands looked malnourished. He was actually about forty-five years old with salt and pepper hair; piercing, playful eyes; and a light shadow of a beard. I trusted his deep eyes, which is important for a woman traveling alone, or else I would have voided the trip right there and then. I always go with my instincts. All six of the deckhands waved hello to me and began to chat among themselves in Guaraní and some Spanish. My journey on Río Paraguay with seven men began.

As we sailed away from Asunción, I watched the bustling pier, the crowds, horse-drawn carriages, and fume-belching vehicles all shrinking. The sound of the city faded as the gateway to Mother Nature was consumed with birds chirping, monkeys howling, and macaws calling. The boat engine was soft, its bow parting the murky, reddish-brown water. The ripples of tiny waves scattered the mosquitoes on the surface, sending them to seek refuge on top of the flat, green leaves of the purple water lilies.

In the evening, I followed the scent of burnt firewood coming from the other side of the ship. As I approached the kitchen, I heard the clanking of pots and pans. The kitchen was in an open area; two oil lamps dangled from the wooden roof. A huge thrush of green plantains hung in the kitchen, and bags of rooted vegetables of *malanga* and colorful tamarillo lay open in an orange plastic bowl. The fire pit sat in the middle on top of some concrete with a heavy wire crate for a burner. A cauldron was suspended by a pair of iron pokes, along with a large, heavy black and greasy-looking pan. Several chipped, beaten-up enamel bowls sat at the side; two large pieces of bloody red steaks occupied one bowl. The flies seemed to have first dibs at our dinner.

Rafael invited me to sit down and immediately gave me the large bowl filled with flour and a cup of water. He motioned for me to knead the flour and I began. He said that we were going to make empanadas.

I began to knead the flour, and the tiny bugs hovering around the oil lamps eventually made their way into the sticky dough. By the time I finished kneading the dough, it looked like I had added a teaspoon. of black sesame seeds. Rafael smiled and said it would be tastier. He handed me an empty Coke bottle as the rolling pin. I rolled out the dough into an odd shape that resembled South America.

Rafael placed the heavy pan on the wire burner and waited for it to heat up. He added the steaks, searing them on both sides for a few seconds. He removed the steaks and placed them back in the same bloody enamel bowl. To the pan, he added big pinches of shallots, garlic, and a handful of mashed beans sprinkled with salt and pepper.

After the mixture was sautéed, he added the steak back to the pan and asked me to carefully lay my dough on top. He covered it with the heavy lid and surrounded it with the red-hot coals.

Dinner with the men was delightful. We cut the empanadas into square wedges. The juice from the tender pieces of steak blended well with the beans, creating a mouthful of savories with a crisp finish from the baked dough, insects and all.

EMPANADAS RÍO PARAGUAY–STYLE

{ makes 10 to 15 empanadas; serves 6 to 8 }

You can almost never go wrong with an empanada, especially since the fillings for these sweet or savory turnovers can be just about whatever your heart desires. In fact, this recipe was inspired by a sensual journey down the Río Paraguay, a trip I will never forget.

3 Tbsp extra-virgin olive oil

1 lb beef tenderloin, finely diced but not minced

Sea salt

Freshly ground black pepper

1 medium white onion, chopped

1 Tbsp minced garlic

1 tsp ground cumin

1 small jalapeño, seeded and finely chopped

¾ cup canned black beans, drained, rinsed, and lightly mashed

1 Tbsp tomato paste

½ cup finely diced celery

2 Tbsp chopped fresh parsley

½ cup beef or vegetable stock

Two 10-count package empanada wrappers (*about 6 inches in diameter*), thawed if frozen

1. In a large nonstick skillet, heat the oil over high heat. In a bowl, season the diced steak with salt and pepper. Add the steak to the skillet and cook for 1 or 2 minutes or until it turns a bit brown. Remove from the pan and set aside.

2. Reduce the heat to low and add the onion, garlic, cumin, and jalapeño. Sauté until the onion is soft, about 3 minutes. Add the beans, tomato paste, celery, and parsley and cook for 3 minutes more. Add the beef and stock, season with more salt and pepper, and continue to cook until mixture is very thick, 4 to 5 minutes more. Remove from the heat and set aside to cool.

3. On a clean cutting board, lay one empanada wrapper. Place about 3 Tbsp of the beef mixture on wrapper. Moisten the edges of the wrapper with water and fold over to form a semicircle, then crimp with a fork. Make more empanadas in same manner.

4. In a heavy skillet over medium heat, slowly heat enough oil for deep-frying (about 3 inches) until a deep-fry thermometer reads 365°F.

5. Fry the empanadas two at a time, turning once, until crisp and golden, 4 to 6 minutes per batch.

6. Transfer to drain on a plate lined with paper towels. Serve warm.

My bed was a burlap hammock with a patched-up blue mosquito net. My "cabin," a windowless single wall of raw, unshaven lumber, faced the starboard (right) side of the riverboat. On one side was a curtain made with beads; behind it was my urine-stained toilet, a hole in the deck. On the other side of my cabin was one of the deckhand's hammock.

In the morning I woke up to laughter. I lay awake in the hammock and looked at the villages passing by. Goats feasted on flower gardens. Naked children chased one another while others waved at me. Men sat on the riverbanks discussing village gossip.

A few villages later, the river bend opened up to dense forest banks. I got up, followed Rafael's laughter, and saw that he had already caught a few river fish. Captain Serg was looking handsome as ever standing by the wheel. Rafael asked if I wanted to help, and I gladly said yes, thinking he was going to give me the fishing rod. Instead he gave me yet another bowl, this time with a knife and a few fish. All the men, including Serg, burst out in loud laughter like schoolgirls.

Rafael said that we were going to make roasted catfish, *malanga*, and tamarillo. This would be breakfast, with yerba maté. We roasted the fish in plantain leaves and mashed up the *malanga* like potatoes.

After the meal, the men showed me pictures of their wives and children and looked at my guidebook for their villages. I asked Serge if he had a wife; he avoided the question with a shy smile.

CORNMEAL-ENCRUSTED BAKED CATFISH

{ serves 4 to 6 }

Here is another unforgettable meal from my trip down the Río Paraguay. I was on my way to Concepción, and eventually to Brazil. Use the freshest fish you can find, preferably right from the source, for that truly authentic riverside experience. Serve hot with Roasted Tamarillos and Purple Potatoes (see page 254).

2 lb catfish fillets, cut into 2-inch strips

1 Tbsp freshly squeezed lime juice

¾ cup yellow cornmeal

¼ cup all-purpose flour

1 Tbsp sweet paprika

1 tsp cayenne pepper

1 Tbsp finely chopped fresh parsley

Sea salt

Freshly ground black pepper

1. Preheat the oven to 400°F. Grease a large baking sheet.

2. Mix the catfish and lime juice in a medium bowl. Set aside.

3. In a small bowl combine cornmeal, flour, paprika, cayenne, parsley, 1½ tsp salt, and 1 tsp pepper. Add the cornmeal mixture to the bowl with the catfish and toss until well coated.

4. Shake off any excess coating and transfer the fish to the baking sheet. Place the fillets in single layer. Reduce the oven temperature to 375°F and bake the fish until firm, 18 to 20 minutes. Season while hot with more salt and pepper.

ROASTED TAMARILLOS & PURPLE POTATOES

{ serves 4 to 6 }

Native to South America, both tamarillos and purple potatoes—especially together—make a great, simple side dish to just about any main course from the continent. Make these for a perfect compliment to Cornmeal-Encrusted Baked Catfish (page 253).

1 lb whole tamarillos
(about 6)

1 lb small purple potatoes,
scrubbed and cut into 1-inch
cubes or halved

Sea salt

2 Tbsp extra-virgin olive oil

Coarsely ground black
pepper

1. Preheat the oven to 400°F. Grease a medium baking sheet.

2. In a large saucepan combine the tamarillos (with stems on) and potatoes. Add a pinch of salt and add enough cold water to cover by 1 inch. Bring to a boil and cook for 5 minutes over medium heat. Drain and let cool.

3. Transfer the potatoes to the prepared baking sheet. Add the olive oil and sprinkle with salt and pepper. Toss lightly.

4. Peel away and discard the skin from the tamarillos, cutting a small slit at the bottoms and leaving the stems intact. Add the tamarillos to the baking sheet with potatoes. Toss both the potatoes and tamarillos once, just to coat, then arrange them in a single layer.

5. Reduce the oven temperature to 375°F and transfer the baking sheet to the oven. Bake 18 to 20 minutes. Season with more salt and pepper and serve immediately.

INDEX

TABLE OF EQUIVALENTS

The exact equivalents in the following tables have been rounded for convenience.

LIQUID / DRY MEASUREMENTS

u.s.	metric
¼ teaspoon	1.25 milliliters
½ teaspoon	2.5 milliliters
1 teaspoon	5 milliliters
1 Tablespoon (3 teaspoons)	15 milliliters
1 fluid ounce (2 Tablespoons)	30 milliliters
¼ cup	60 milliliters
⅓ cup	80 milliliters
½ cup	120 milliliters
1 cup	240 milliliters
1 pint (2 cups)	480 milliliters
1 quart (4 cups, 32 ounces)	960 milliliters
1 gallon (4 quarts)	3.84 liters
1 ounce (by weight)	28 grams
1 pound	448 grams
2.2 pounds	1 kilogram

OVEN TEMPERATURE

fahrenheit	celsius	gas
250	120	½
275	140	1
300	150	2
325	160	3
350	180	4
375	190	5
400	200	6
425	220	7
450	230	8
475	240	9
500	260	10

LENGTHS

u.s.	metric
⅛ inch	3 millimeters
¼ inch	6 millimeters
½ inch	12 millimeters
1 inch	2.5 centimeters